LOVING GOD PRACTICALLY

A Blueprint for Living

Nancy Andreson

DEDICATION AND ACKNOWLEDGEMENTS

This book is dedicated to: Sharon Sterrenburg Roy and Elizabeth McGregor Priscilla Barber All four mentored me in loving God. Each sowed into a particular season of my early journey. They were lovers of God in ways that spoke volumes to many, yet none was famous. Each of them had a life marked by faithfulness, humility, courage, and prayer. They taught me what it was to practice for eternity, while living here on earth. Each now beholds Him face to face. I would not be who I am without the fingerprints of their faith.

I also want to acknowledge and sincerely thank the people who helped me in this project. All are God given gifts.

To Pat Larson. You tenderly keep me honest! Thank you for your prays all along the way. Thanks for faithfully reading each chapter as I wrote it, feeding back, encouraging me, making suggestions and cheering me on. I thank God for our friendship.

To Tiffany Taves, you are a precious treasure in the kingdom. Without your gift of time, your amazing talent, suggestions and encouragement I would not have gone on to edit again and again and again.

To my husband, Don, who patiently and sympathetically listened to my complaints in the process of writing. On the bad weeks when I wondered if I had anything of value to say and was convinced the entire idea of writing was foolishness, your compassion, optimism, sympathy and encouragement kept me going for one more week.

To Leavitt Andreson, my daughter-in-love. You are a genius at following my sometimes confused sense of order. You never make fun of me, rather always have a smile on your face and a kind word, as you take on one more administrative task. Where would I be without you.

Thanks be to God! He gave me the life I have and made me the person I am with plenty of weaknesses to boast in! Anything you find helpful in these pages, credit goes to Him. The book has been a partnership that consisted of our many conversations, writing, rewriting, praying, listening, rewriting and rewriting. I can't believe we've done it! Let's do it again!

To my readers: My hope and prayer is that as you read, you'll feel encouraged to never stop growing in God.

Table of Contents

Preface
Introduction
Chapter 1
  Foolish, Weak, Unqualified Beginnings   13
Chapter 2
  Whom Do I Worship?   24
Chapter 3
  Peace With God   31
Chapter 4
  Love Comes Softly   42
Chapter 5
  Intimacy With God   50
Chapter 6
  Becoming Authentic   59
Chapter 7
  God Adventures in Everyday Life   69
Chapter 8
  What About the Bible?   78
Chapter 9
  Belief or Relationship?   90
Chapter 10
  Keeping It Fresh   98
Chapter 11
  Growing   109
Chapter 12
  Adopted in Love - A Journey of Change   123
Conclusion
  Isaiah 5 5   128

Preface

I've been up and I've been down
I've done life on a merry go round.
I've skinned my knees many a time,
And had my life change on the turn of a dime.

I've lived where giraffe and lion stride free,
Raced alongside Ostrich in the Rift Valley.
I've worshipped with gypsies under the stars,
Drunk hard cider from barrels in real Basque bars.

I've cried enough tears to fill a swimming pool,
Am thankful God treasures each drop as a jewel.
I've forever friends become distant memories,
As their lives grew beyond their friendship of me.

I've walked the streets of Bethlehem,
Tasted the colors and sounds of Jerusalem,
Been baptized in the Jordan River,
Sung a solo to God in the Church of the Holy Sepulcher.

I've crept watchfully on the tightrope of faith,
Escaping the chasm of fear that awaited.
I've abounded in faith – when all things were at hand,
So know well how that roadway narrows and expands.

I know: "The Lord is my Shepherd, I have all that I need",
As I've closed my eyes and let God carry me.
I've walked beside death more than once
And have soldiers who guard how my heart pumps.

I've prayed through a nation that is not my own,
Seen God do multiple miracles as his name was enthroned.
I've gained a heart family and a child, or a few,
Who've colored my life with wonderful rich hues.

I've known joy that is way beyond belief,
And been swallowed by seasons of unrelenting grief.
I've known storms it took all my strength to stand.
And times I was carried sleeping inside of God's hand.

We've had times when milk came via child's piggy banks,
And undeserved abundance that's inspired deep thanks.

I've certainly given up a home once, twice, three times then four
And seen God open a better, but not always easy, new door.

There's so much more that remains unsaid,
Tales of adventures that echo in my head.
Life's ups and downs, ins and outs -
A testimony of God's presence that so clearly shouts.

Each line in our lives is a chapter, some a book.
All mark crossroads of paths that we've took.
Times we've had choices to trust, worship and pray
That some new lesson of God's making, might stay.

I am no gifted poet, this is clearly seen.
I'm simply a servant child of a great mighty King.
He knows me, chose me, and firmly holds me,
Sent Jesus to secure me by hanging on a tree.

How can we not love him all the days of our life?
How can we not treasure Him as the source of our life?
How can we not give Him our hands, heart and feet?
How could we not create arenas for us to meet?

Oh God, give us an appetite to know you more
To stand in your presence and knock at your door.
To wait for your presence, your thoughts so to hear
To tell you our secrets, and give you our fear.

Oh God how we need you, to walk by our side,
You are the Great Teacher, your heart you don't hide.
You've said if we ask you – you'll abundantly give,
And Father we believe you – it's your desire we live.

So Father I give you my heart as I read,
And ask that you'll speak the things I most need.
Be it gold dust or a nugget, both leave the same,
Something of value that buys "fruit that remains."

Oh Lord, do not let me leave these pages unchanged,
Let this be a meeting that You have arranged.

In Jesus Name - Amen

INTRODUCTION

I am someone who came to writing later in life. I don't recall when it happened but one day I realized this is something I can do, and I enjoy it as much as teaching in person. Writing a book however is very different than writing an article. It is way above my pay scale or experienced gifting.

I am a person who has always had much to say about many things. I grew up being silenced and being told I was stupid. When I was filled with the Holy Spirit, I suddenly felt my voice and life empowered by the love of God. I went from being very quiet and shy, to sharing fairly strongly what I thought about most everything. I think God was smiling and saying to himself, "Look what love will do." To say I highly esteemed my new freedom would be an understatement. I had a silent dad and an over-expressive mom. I went from being silent to over-expressive, and that was how I functioned for many years. Perhaps about 10 years ago, I felt like God asked me to be quiet. And so I went from being in front in many meetings, to holding my tongue and taking a back seat. I don't want to give you the wrong impression. I didn't stop talking altogether, nor did I stop teaching or pastoring. I simply backed way down and in some settings I took the back row. It was good for me.

Then 3 years ago for no apparent reason, I felt like God said, I want you to talk now, and I want you to write a book. That was confirmed in some very interesting ways by people in different settings who do not know me. Writing a book is not something I have ever wanted to do. It's taken me 3 years of stops, starts and endless rewrites to finish.

God sometimes asks us to do things that to us seem impossible. To handle it, I thought of it as writing small essays about some very important lessons on loving God. I also found great comfort in telling myself the outcome wasn't in my hands. I have done many things God has asked me to do thinking it was to one end. To my shock God used it entirely differently. I have learned that when God asks us to do something, it's best to say yes. It is always an invitation to obedience and often an invitation to joy. This time I did! The only thing I had to lose was pride if I failed. Sometimes that is exactly what God is after. Our failures are often stops on the roadmap of our life. They become sign posts to expanded understanding and new experiences we'd not looked for or seen before. What I had to gain from saying yes was the treasure that comes from a deeper trust and dependence on him. That is something that is priceless. When Peter stepped out on the water he had to keep his eyes on Jesus. As long as he did that he was fine. I don't see Peter's experience as a failure, I see it as a sign of what is possible.

For this gal who barely graduated from high school and doesn't understand the rules behind grammar, writing this book has been like walking on water. I have reached the end of this invitation and my feet are still dry.

It is said that every person has a life message. If I were to narrow mine down to just one theme it would be: practically loving God every day. It has kept me going in the bad, good, confusing, challenging, victorious and joy filled every-days, each of us participates in. It's something I have fought for and applied to every area of my life. It's a lifestyle I would want to hand onto my children, children-in-love, grandchildren, great grandchildren, and their children. It is something I would love to be known for by my friends, and my enemies.

Of course we can't love God and not love people. That is the other side of my story. I've learned much and pray what I have learned will spark some new thoughts as you and your Heavenly Father write your story. If you laugh or cry and if you walk away with some small gold nugget that encourages you – then this three year endeavor will have been a seed I am doubly glad I have had the privilege living and planting.

"Remember, dear brothers and sisters that few of you were wise in the world's eyes or powerful or wealthy when God called you. Instead, God chose things the world considers foolish in order to shame those who think they are wise. And He chose things that are powerless to shame those who are powerful. God chose things despised by the world, things counted as nothing at all and used them to bring to nothing the things the world considers important. As a result no one can ever boast in the presence of God."

1 CORINTHIANS 1:26-29

1

FOOLISH, WEAK, QUALIFIED BEGINNINGS

Often in reviewing one's beginning you will see a seed of what will grow over time. It is surely true in my case. My beginnings were foolish, weak and felt despised. My name, Nancy, in Hebrew means grace. It perfectly describes my life as long as you add one very important word in front of it. God! My life is a testimony of God's grace.

I hated my name as a child. I'd moved 17 times by age 16. One year as I entered a new school, I decided to introduce myself as Ginger! It worked pretty well until I began to make a few friends who would call me on the phone and ask for Ginger. My parents would promptly hang up the phone after telling the caller there was no one there by that name. I dared not share I was the person they were looking for. Instead I began hanging out close to the phone all the time to intercept all calls. That seemed to work for a while. The trouble I was trying to avoid overtook me at the first parent teacher conference when the teacher referred to me as Ginger! If that was not enough to seal my fate, there was the totally identifiable handwriting on school work with the name Ginger Memory written at the top of each page. They refused to support my new identity and informed my teacher of my proper name. I knew what was coming when they returned home and hoped they would understand. Instead they grounded me (which also included loss of phone privileges) for a long time. I was told they named me Nancy because that was a name they loved and that was who I was.

I had to abandon my not so well thought out plan and explain to my friends Ginger was my nickname but that my parents wouldn't take their calls if they used that name. Everyone called me Nancy once the teacher followed the wishes of my parents and began calling me by my given name.

I often wonder what attracted me to the name Ginger. Over the years, I've surmised it related to two things: I wanted to be unique. Even more I wanted to reinvent my personality. Nancy was a very popular name – in fact one year there were 4 of us in the same classroom. No one had the name Ginger! I was exceedingly shy, a wallflower, a poor student, always the shortest person in the class, and so thin it was pitiful. Add curly long hair (not the style) and I was miserable in heart. I had the confidence of a very small pea and longed to add some spice to my surroundings, to be athletic, full of confidence, a great student and thought of as competent and a leader. Who ever heard of a pea named Ginger – the name simply sparkles. If you move every year, it offers you opportunities others don't have – so somewhere in the midst of another move, I found some courage to come up with a fail-safe plan to reinvent me. Instead it affirmed the failure I always felt myself to be.

I had no idea my life looked very different to God. He saw me as a perfect blackboard to write the story of His Grace upon. A story that He continues to write even now.

My dad was in the Navy. We moved from military base to military base. That was normal life – I usually lived in military housing. In my reality everyone moved. If it wasn't us, it was the neighbors who got new "orders." We were all nomads. For me the result of being a nomad was an insular life. I learned to be alone. There are no lasting or deep friendships in my history. At one point I invented an imaginary rabbit who was my friend. He lived in a box beneath our kitchen sink. I would faithfully feed him each morning before going to school. After school I'd take him to my bedroom where we'd hang out and have long conversations. Every night I'd tuck him back in his box under the kitchen sink and tell him to have sweet dreams. My parents tolerated this far better than when I changed my name to Ginger!

I was the first of 4 daughters. I had twin sisters who were 2 1/2 years younger. The only time they got along with me was when they were fighting with one another. Their personalities were opposites of mine: non-compliant, extroverts, risk takers who were in trouble all of the time. They were simply allergic to the concept of obedience. No amount of discipline would remedy their condition. The very word seemed an invitation to do the opposite. They delighted in causing trouble in whatever situation they were in. I am not telling you anything they would not say themselves.

Every night my dad would climb the stairs twice to spank them. Twice because one time wasn't enough to curb their mischief. They would actually get 3 spankings a night: one because of some mischief, one because before my dad could descend the stairs they would be laughing at him for spanking them, then a final one which would take care of the next mischief of the night. They loved sneaking into my bedroom to scare the heck out of me. They did their very best to be hateful towards me both physically and verbally. It took them well into adulthood to apologize for how hard they made life. They were also a terror to all the children in the neighborhoods we lived in. (Only one twin is now alive, but she would tell you this is true.) This again reinforced my feeling of being alone in childhood.

I also had a delightful little sister who was born when I was 10. As a little girl, she had the most tender of hearts. She gave us all such joy. If she even suspected she had made you angry it was enough to cause her to burst into tears. The highlight of every school day was returning home to be greeted by her screams of delight at my presence. I loved sharing my bedroom with her. We were very close as children. She'd call me mom when mom wasn't around. It took till I was 10, but finally I had some company. I trace the beginning of my training in motherhood to her birth.

I could write an entire book about each of my parents. For the sake of space and kindness – let me keep it brief. They didn't get along. They were both strong disciplinarians. Neither was a church goer. My mom – an extreme extrovert – had an explosive temper, was abusive, and was always right. I came to believe she suffered from mental illness. I don't think I will ever appreciate the challenges she faced internally. My dad – an extreme introvert – was faithful and loyal to family, creative with his hands, a hard worker, never used profanity, loved rules, and didn't use many words. Love and emotion were tightly reigned in. He strongly believed we should be self-taught. This caused me countless tears when he would refuse to help me grasp math or spelling. His favorite saying was, "figure it out yourself," honestly believing he was helping to prepare me for life. He also inspected every chore we were given to make sure it had been performed perfectly. He loved the structure of the military and he loved that he could keep changing fields (which meant we would move for his schooling and then move again for placement in his new field of expertise). After he died, we learned from a counselor he most certainly suffered from an attachment disorder that could be traced back to an ill mother who died when he was 1. If he didn't like something or someone – he'd move. When we found this out it was as if a puzzle piece had been handed to us. It helped both my sisters and step siblings understand the behavior patterns of his entire life.

My parents separated and then divorced when I was 17. I lived with my mother for 2 intolerable years from 16 to 18. It was when I was 16 that my life began to have a bright spot. This was through the care and testimony of a wonderful Christian doctor by the name of Dr. Van Valen. I met him because of a medical procedure I needed. For some unknown reason to me, he and his wonderful family took me under their wing and introduced me to a living relationship with God. I didn't live with them; they simply adopted me as extended family. It was under their care that I began to have an adult understanding of what it meant to follow Jesus. At a college camp for youth, which they paid for me to attend, I intentionally gave my heart and life to Jesus. I left home ON my 18th birthday – moving to Hollywood, California to begin attending Hollywood Presbyterian Church. For a short while I attended a Community College, but dropped out when finances and transportation became an insurmountable issue. I then began working full time at a bank.

18 was a pivotal year in my life. I left home, became financially independent, began attending a church regularly, got involved in the college department of the church, moved in with a Christian girl who was actually named Ginger, got baptized in the Holy Spirit, met my husband, got married, and by my 19th birthday had been serving in Africa next to him as a missionary for an entire month! I still – over 50 years later – can hardly wrap my mind around what happened. The decision to leave home and follow Jesus was like I'd hitched myself to the tail of a 747 in flight.

For as long as I remember I believed strongly in God. Where this belief came from remains a mystery to me. (Remember Grace?) As a young child, my dad hated religion, my mom professed to being Catholic – but she didn't know much of what Catholics believed. She never attended Catholic Church. There had been a Catholic priest who had treated her kindly in her childhood which had been her only connection to the church. Neither of my parents was familiar with the Bible. We didn't go to church when I was young. Yet without introduction or teaching, I believed in God, and I talked to Him all the time. It would be perfectly truthful to say my life was filled with conversations with God, (they preceded my friend the rabbit by many years). From somewhere a Children's Bible appeared in my home, (grace) and I claimed it. Perhaps some unnamed person gave it to me as a gift? It had cartoon drawings of scenes from the Bible with captions underneath them. It was my favorite book. I would spend hours at night savoring the pictures. I loved to pray. At some point that book disappeared. I have no idea what happened to it – perhaps it was lost in a move.

I also had visions of Jesus' return. They would happen at night when I would close my eyes. I would imagine/see Jesus returning to earth. The sky was filled with white clouds which would part – He would be on a huge white horse. He was clothed in white robes and had white flowing hair and He would have a sword drawn – but He never looked angry, not like He was coming to fight a war – rather He was coming in victory. He simply looked determined and very strong. Myriads of angels and people would be in His train. Many of them were also on horses; some just seemed to float on their own accord. It was spectacular.

This vision/picture would always provoke the same simple prayer: "Lord would you let me live to see that day? I want to be alive when you return. I want to see you come back! Please don't let me die before then." Then I would expand my prayer and add, "I also want you to let me live long enough to get married." My remembrance of this predates kindergarten – perhaps around age 3 or 4.

Those were my two repetitive prayers. Both were spoken directly to God. I also knew I had an angel that watched over me. I never saw him but I found this very comforting. I don't remember much about my other conversations with God. Only that I was always talking to Him, always aware of His presence.

I forgave my mother many years ago. What I say about her is not in anger or to dishonor her – she gave me all she had. She gave her life to Jesus later in life and so like me received forgiveness for all she did. I share what I do, because it is an important part of MY story. Her explosive temper and her belief that she was always right were a bad combination to be on the other end of. This worked its way into my prayer life. I believed in God strongly – and as a result, I always wanted to please Him. I knew He was a greater authority than my mom. I knew lying to be wrong – something that didn't please Him. When conflict developed with my mother due to something she wrongly thought I was guilty of doing, she and I would have a battle of wills. I think I got my strength genes from both her and my dad. She was determined that I should confess and be saved from becoming a liar. I was determined not to disappoint God by lying. It never ended well for me. I'd end up confessing to something I'd not done, to stop my accidental death at her hands. Then I would spend hours telling God how sorry I was for disappointing Him and vowing to not lie the next time this scene repeated itself. Somehow from this cauldron of fire my love for truth seemed to emerge.

For me, God was as real and as much a person as my parents. He just lived somewhere else and He could hear and see me all the time. I was in my 20's when God clearly addressed the circumstance I'd grown up in. His words healed my heart, changed my mind, and became foundational to how I now understand God's view of failure. More about this in a later chapter.

I did have an uncle that came to visit us from Missouri one time. I spent almost all of my childhood years in California. I don't recall ever meeting him prior to his visit. I remember I was in 3rd grade and we lived in military housing in Vallejo, California. He was a Lutheran pastor. He asked my parents if he could baptize us children, and they gave their permission. He baptized us in our kitchen sink. As he sprinkled water on us in the name of the

Father, Son and Holy Ghost, I felt an enormous wave of peace and joy sweep over me. It was so intense I began to cry tears of joy. I also felt incredible relief. That moment I *knew* God had sent this man to perform the ceremony that indicated God had accepted me as part of His family.

For me, there was no question of accepting God. I had always accepted Him, always believed, and always wanted to please Him. The question was on God's side. Did He accept me? Had I made the grade? Baptism by this Holy Man proved to me I was in. As I matured into an adult believer I was re-baptized, but I will always treasure my first baptism. Although my theology wasn't correct, and I did not understand what was happening, I have no doubt something beautiful, filled with love and deeply spiritual was sealed between God and me that day.

After we were baptized my parents briefly decided to go to church. For perhaps 4 months we attended a Baptist church. What I remember was that the pastor yelled quite loudly for long periods of time when he talked about God. Every Sunday we sat behind 4 beautiful blond sisters who had long golden ringlets that would hang over the pew. It was all I could do to resist putting my finger inside a ringlet without them knowing. My sisters were less disciplined and would get slapped or pinched every week by my mom, for touching their hair. Then we moved.

Several years later my dad retired from the military. His first job was on a missile base at Vandenberg Air Force Base. We lived in Santa Maria, California, and my parents decided to go back to church. This time it was a Lutheran church. I was just at the age where you took confirmation classes. I didn't learn much about the Bible in those classes, but it was where I discovered there was a book of prayers written for all kinds of things. Everything you could think of had a prayer written for it. I loved that book. I started praying those prayers. Every time something would come up I would check to see if there was a prayer that had been written for it. That book became my closest my friend. With time however I began to get bored with the prayers. I wasn't satisfied with saying the same things over and over again. The prayers were also so formal which made God seem unfriendly to me. They also put limits on my heart thoughts. These were things that came to my mind that I felt I should say to God. So I began writing my own prayers. I'd spend hours composing written conversations to God. Most every challenge I faced would be turned to a prayer.

During that season, my family had begun saying grace around the table before the evening meal. I would volunteer to pray all the time. My parents had chosen a set prayer I still remember to this day.

> "At this table be our host,
> Father, Son and Holy Ghost.
> Food and drink are from above,
> tokens of His heavenly love. Amen."

They preferred my sisters pray because I would stretch out the set prayer as much as I could get away with. In fact, I began writing my own prayers for grace (not that I was invited to deviate from the authorized version of "grace"). In my mind, this was the only time we prayed as a family and we needed to get as much into it as possible. I didn't think anyone else in our family prayed, so I became the self-appointed spokesperson for what I thought we should be talking to God about. I passionately believed that God heard and answered prayer. In my mind, it was important for our family to ask Him to bless us and the world around us, not just our food!

One time we were company at someone else's house for Thanksgiving. I had been asking God to give me the honor of saying grace for that special occasion. I was prepared should He say yes to my request. I had my prayer composed on paper in my pocket! It makes me laugh now. You can't make this stuff up. Sure enough our host asked me to say grace. I prayed so long and so sincerely that my mom kicked me under the table to get me to stop. I ignored her first kick because I hadn't come to the end of my written prayer. She made sure I couldn't ignore the second kick!

As I aged into my older teen years, I became cynical of God. I never stopped believing in Him, but life was just very hard and many things happened that deeply wounded my spirit.

My parent's relationship which always had been difficult, descended into a hell. As the oldest, and being a super responsible child, a lot of pressure was on me. My mom thought of herself as a Christian but led a radically un-Christian life. She used Bible verses to control me, and so at some point I decided if God was like my mom, and if these verses she used were true, I didn't like God and I didn't want to follow Him. It was not until being loved by Dr. Van Valen's family, and attending a youth camp they paid for me to attend, that God broke through. I broke down before the leaders and described the things my mom was involved in as a Christian and how I could not follow God as a result. The leaders opened the bible and pointed out to me specific verses that revealed God had as much of a problem with her behavior as I did! She wasn't following Him. It was then that I decided my life was a mess, and that I had nothing to lose by re-dedicating myself to Jesus.

I also knew at that moment I had to leave my home as soon as possible. Little did I know the hell I would go through when I re-dedicated my life to Jesus. Life would have been much easier during those last weeks at home had I chosen to become a prostitute, a Hell's Angel, a drug dealer or a heroin addict. I know this to be true as those were choices others in my family made. It wasn't that their choices were approved of either, but they weren't taken as a direct insult to mom. To this day I believe God preserved my life during that passage.

Our stories are important. I have come to appreciate how precious each one is. I didn't come to be a "pray-er" by myself. It happened <u>to</u> me or <u>in</u> me. I believe I was born with an appetite for God and for prayer. It was part of my DNA or my destiny. I didn't earn it; I didn't deserve it; and I didn't work for it. It was just part of me. I don't think it makes me a better person than someone else. I also don't think I'll be rewarded for it. How can you be rewarded for something you didn't create within yourself? I could not have gotten here on my own. It was by grace – God's grace. I believe that He made sure I received my Hebrew name, the one I attempted to reject.

Each of us has our own story. I have met so many who have had sovereign beginnings with God. My story is unique to me, but it is not unusual. God loves us and His grace surrounds us all. One of my sisters, who came to faith quite late in life after much heartbreak, devastation and self-abuse has a very different story than mine. It too, is filled with His grace. My four children, every one growing up in a radically loving Christian home, has a unique story filled with God's grace. I have come to believe God's grace isn't for a few special ones who particularly need it. Grace is who He is. When He is present so is grace. We all need it. He abundantly showers it on us. It is always grace that leads us to His throne.

I hope you will take some time to look for His grace in your beginnings. If they aren't apparent at first, ask Him to show you where He was working in your life back then. Then ask Him where He is working now. We never ever outgrow our need for grace. He never tires of delighting to introduce us to its unlimited depths.

Rise up oh man of God, be done with lesser things. Give heart and soul and strength and mind, to serve the King of Kings.

WILLIAM P. MERRILL

2

WHOM DO I WORSHIP?

A my Grant recorded in a song: "Life is Hard and It Might Not Get Easier". At one point that was one of my favorite sayings. Life is complicated and often not easy to figure out. Who we are centered on makes all the difference. Life is easier if we have the abundant grace, strength and patience that comes from God – but sometimes that slips through our fingers along the way.

When I was a child things were easier. As children our job is mostly to follow the directions of those older than us. Go to school, do your homework, clean your room, do your chores, say you are sorry, play nice, tell the truth, stay out of trouble, eat the food that is put before you without complaint, show gratitude, be kind, wash your hands and brush your teeth. I am not saying these things are easy to do as a kid, because some of them are things we still have trouble accomplishing as adults!

As you transition into adulthood the people who have had responsibility in your life transition to advisors/helpers. Ultimately you're the one in charge of your destiny. Often we rush to be in charge of our destiny before we want the responsibility that comes with those changes.

Living life it can seem like things move slowly, but think of the changes that happen in a few short years. We learn how central money is to life. In the transition from dependence to independence, we must figure out how we will make a living, define a career path, and prepare for it. We need housing, utilities, furniture, transportation, food. We embrace the word "bills" as part of life.

All too often debt can end up running our life decisions, unless we come from a privileged background, have generous parents, happened upon a well-paying first job, or are an extremely self-disciplined person who plans well in advance.

Once fully independent you are the one who has to purchase the food, prepare the food, clean the house, work the job and have a social life. If we have pets they need walking, feeding, picking up after. It gets really exciting when you add a spouse and have the tension that comes as you work out the blessings and challenges of the new relationship.

Should you choose to delay marriage because you want to focus on your career – you will likely be very busy with much responsibility and stress in your work.

Should we have children they become the highest of priorities. We have traded places with our parents. Resources are stretched thinner. What we will pay just for diapers for 2 children, would pay for a very nice vacation in the Caribbean! We are responsible to discipline, entertain, and clothe the kids. We settle their squabbles, make sure they do their homework, get them to their activities on time, pay for childcare, and on it goes.... Where does time go? And what about energy? If you are single parenting all of this is greatly compounded.

This transition can take a decade for some, maybe 15 years for others, some are thrown into it. At 18, I left home, got a job in the city, rode a bus daily then hoofed it to and from work or my apartment, ate lots of pickles and hot peppers, cereal, and peanut butter. I was supported by no one but God. By 19, I was married and a missionary in Africa.

My point is: becoming independent is a learning curve. The time and skill it takes is significantly more than your child-hood chores. The patterns of our childhood change. With those changes, our relationship with God must mature as well. We need God's grace and strength, but it's easy to lose perspective and time with Him when we are so busy simply learning new life skills. Time with Him can slip through our fingers because He isn't in our face making demands, sending bills in the mail, or competing with our need for down time. Of course the very issue of learning new life skills can drive us to God, when we realize we are in over our heads and need help!

If you came to Jesus after childhood, you can tend to fit God in as an additional puzzle piece of the established patterns of your life. Yet life with Him every day is the most important thing we can do. How do we keep Him first?

It isn't by having His abstract presence with us, nor by giving mental and verbal assent to the fact that God is God and is all around us all of the time, while we do our best to live honorably and keep up with the demands of life.

It is not sufficient to believe IN God and go to church. The answer is so simple and non-profound that writing it down seems fool-ish! Keeping Him first comes by building a LIFESTYLE that en-folds the presence of His personhood in all we do. That has been the blueprint I have adopted for living.

Lifestyles can be dictated by our culture, our responsibilities, crises, the voices of people who feel they own us, career and even ministry. They can also be dictated by the grace and voice of God. I need Him in the middle of my responsibilities, my relationships, my mountaintop joys, my tensions and crises, every day. For me, not relegating Him to a category of my life, but rather building my lifestyle around His Presence, has been the key to genuinely loving Him and others. It has also allowed me to lay hold of His grace, strength, and love in the midst of some very rocky times.

It has helped me to compare this to the solar system in which we live. The sun is at the center and its gravitational pull holds each planet in its place. I know that is very simplistic – but I need simple. When I keep God at my center and gravitate around His presence, then when a day, month, or year feels like either summer or winter, His love holds me and keeps me on track. When I don't do this, but rather live like I expect God to be the one who gravitates around the center of my demands, schedule, needs, and moods, these lesser things become what dictates my very erratic life patterns.

God doesn't give up on me. His love and grace never stop – but I can't maintain the effectiveness and direction His love and presence are meant to bring because my focus is on me and my circumstances rather than on His presence. I tend to either drift through my days or I get lost in the emotions that drive my own agenda. My lifestyle reverts to me, the demands of my schedule, my circle of needs, the circle of needs of those close to me, my moods and preferences.

Jesus absolutely does call us to love ourselves. I am not saying we are to ignore self-care, yet it is always in the context of loving Him first. By putting Him first, front and center, He directs my self-care. Self-care becomes an act of loving obedience. I dislike being black or white, but we either create a lifestyle with God as the center or we don't. Remember the grace part here… it is a learning curve that takes time. It's like riding a bike, we don't do it perfectly from the start. Even the best experienced riders have wipeouts from time to time. We all need God's grace.

Lifestyle does not make me a Christian or not a Christian. Faith in Jesus and His work on the cross does. We are saved by grace! Rather, lifestyle reveals what I believe. What lifestyle displays are my values. Am I a Christ centered Christian whose loyalties are not divided? Then I more easily lend my eyes, ears, heart, and thoughts to enjoying His presence and counsel because I am honoring His presence in the midst of the everyday.

It can be helpful to take time to think about this issue. As I have done this, I have discovered something logical and profound. What I worship is at the center of my lifestyle. Going back to the illustration of the solar system, what we worship is our sun. Do I worship myself (my needs, my desires)? Do I worship something other than God? A hard question I ask myself regularly is, whom do I worship? There are seasons when it is helpful for me to reflect on this question almost daily, because I feel so invested in some outcome, I keep taking God's place. (To answer truthfully, I don't depend solely on my own perception of my life – I review the evidence. If my lifestyle demonstrates something other than God, I know I have an "idol" in hiding.) I know I have empowered it. It's not a time for excuses but rather for repentance, a review of the why's behind my heart condition, and a plan for a course correction. This is a process I invite Jesus to sit down in the middle of. I need His grace and help here.

My idols all look pretty attractive, reasonable, and often they seem very worthy. This is why they are sometimes hard to spot. The problem is, they are not the Presence of God Himself. In fact they lead me away from God and they keep me very busy in the process, so I often don't have time to notice them.

Again this is simplistic, but I think of idols as gods full of empty promises. We give them their power through placing them at the center of our world, and then protecting them. That is when their empty promises begin shouting to us. They begin pushing us to do things quickly. We make small and not so small adjustments in our trajectory because our guidance system has a virus.

Idols are empowered competitors for attention and affection. We always feel affection for that which makes us feel secure and meaningful. Here is a natural law: our time and service always naturally flow toward our affections! It is usually a very subtle shift, not happening in a day or a week. We sometimes hardly notice the shift happening. One day we realize God is no longer the sun in our solar system. He now becomes just a planet we visit when we have time or a pressing need. God becomes a temporary fix – or obligation when things seem out of control. I cannot number the times I have heard a person say... I really need to get back to church because life isn't going well. What they are realizing is God is someone they haven't visited for a while. He certainly hasn't been the sun in their life system.

This shift has happened to people far more holy and passionately in love and courageous in God than me. King David was one! God said of him: "Here is a man after my own heart. He will always do what I ask" (Acts 13:22). Somewhere along the line David stopped enjoying God's presence. It was so subtle he didn't recognize it. As a result he ended up in a lifestyle that didn't match his convictions.

It happens all the time. It has happened to me. I am sad to say there have been times I have chosen "lesser things" to center my life on. When it has happened, I end up doing God halfheartedly. What is so incredible and hopeful is that God's presence, grace and love have ALWAYS confronted me, drawn me back and met me in my place of repentance. *I have His unmerited favor in the midst of my failures.* He loves to restore. When God forgives and restores it is like nothing else. There is no residue of condemnation or guilt.

When I was a child, my dad purchased a small piece of land and built a cabin on privately owned property inside of Yosemite National Park. We spent many a vacation there. A small but somewhat high and wide waterfall was not too far from us. At the end of a day of working on the cabin, dad would shout to us children, "Shall we go to the river for a swim or to the waterfall?" I loved that waterfall. I have always compared repentance, forgiveness and restoration to the feeling I would get as I stood under its power. It washed all the dirt and sweat away without any effort on my part. What I needed to do was simply get beneath its water. Then I would lie in its pool of churning effervescence extending the wonderful cleansing process until I felt squeaky clean. I'd return home not just clean, but refreshed and renewed! I was always excited and humbled by that majesty. There is much more majesty in God's forgiveness. It should always take our breath away. I am overwhelmed when I think about how it makes us squeaky clean, refreshed, and refocused on that which brings true life. Like my waterfall, God's forgiveness is available every day. There is no charge; and He cleans unreservedly. That is who He is!

Take time to ask the question: Whom do I worship? Review the evidence of your own lifestyle before you answer. Don't be overly discouraged if you realize it isn't Jesus – rather be encouraged, you are on a growing edge where God Himself will meet you. Simply thoroughly repent and stand in the waterfall of His love and forgiveness. Then sit in the pool of His presence and let it fill you. Listen for His voice. His power will not just cleanse, it will empower, refresh and literally change your desire.

If you are a normal person like me, you will most likely visit this place many times in your journey with God. Sometime from now, when you review your life, you'll see the adjustments God called you to make are unforgettable places you experienced the profound grace, love, and empowering of God. They are often the doorways to a new season of abundant life in Him.

The foundation of the Christian's peace is everlasting; it is what no time, no change can destroy. It will remain when the body dies; it will remain when the mountains depart and the hills shall be removed, and when the heavens shall be rolled together as a scroll. The fountain of His comfort shall never be diminished, and the stream shall never be dried. His comfort and joy is a living spring in the soul, a well of water springing up to everlasting life.

JONATHAN EDWARDS

3

PEACE WITH GOD

C ancer is prevalent in our day. I passionately hate it because it has robbed me of precious friends, family and teachers. When one has cancer normal cells mutate, multiply and eventually if not stopped, cause death. It is a curse that does not come from God.

There is also cancer that eats away at the heart of our relationship with God. It is just as great a robber. I hate the lies that it tells, the sickness it causes, and the way these things multiply in each area of our life. Instead of confidence in God, we feel nibbled at or torn by fear. What is left are holes of uncertainty that make sustained joy in life unattainable. Peace and fear are not good co-inhabitants. For many years my life in God did not allow me to receive the benefits His presence and peace assure.

Most of my early years as a Christian were spent working hard to do the "right things" with "right attitudes" in order to earn his favor. My life was about righteous works connected to a pure heart – so I could be in good standing with God. The theology of "unmerited favor" didn't match my experiential understanding of favor. I regretted the many things I did to disqualify myself from deserving God's favor through sin. Tormented by this quest to earn God's favor, I was terrified of failure, yet I couldn't escape its grasp. I did not know this at the time, but I absolutely believed that "people who failed deserved to be punished." (A phrase taken from the book: *Search for Significance* by Robert McGee.)

Even though I "knew" God loved me and forgave my sin, "knew" that Jesus died on the cross for me, I didn't find freedom or peace in this truth. I didn't apprehend what forgiveness actually meant. In childhood, forgiveness was preceded by painful punishment. That formed my experiential (not theological) understanding of forgiveness and love. When it came to my failure, I often thought of God with an angry face and a raised arm, or with the uncaring, mostly silent, or serious tone of the important people in my childhood. I believed God was always right because he was GOD, not because He was GOD, GOOD, KIND and always AVAILABLE.

Our parents are the best representative of God to His little ones, and because I was positive both of my parents loved me, my understanding of love was wildly distorted. I thought the way they treated me was what love looked like. That wild distorted view became the clothing I dressed God in. In my parent's defense, there are no perfect parents, just better and worse ones. My parents did genuinely love me. Yet every parent is a sinner! Most all of us as adults have to work though some wrong understanding of God as a result of our imperfect models. Certainly each of my 4 children have – and we did a better job of parenting than many.

It's hard to build a lifestyle of loving God when you're at least half afraid of Him. You push into Him, but only when you are pretty sure He isn't angry with you. Because of my past, I believed anger was an expression of love. What I ended up with in the first dozen years of my relationship with God was a schizophrenic relationship. I lived in a place of always wondering if I was or wasn't okay with Him. I imagined awful words and feelings He had towards me when I was doing poorly. I certainly did not live in His provision of abundant peace.

You may not relate to the experience of my earlier years with God. You may have always had a healthy, transparent, rich, two way relationship with Jesus. You are a rare and blessed exception. The majority of us seem to have been touched by a bit of confusion. Apprehending God's love is challenging and most of us fall somewhere on a line of continuum between only slightly confused to very confused. At some time in our lives most are driven to earn His approval by our good behavior. We believe that will open the door to peace with God, as well as earn us the privilege of His reward.

Our culture is one that blesses those who do well and are beautiful. It rejects and shames those who fail. This doesn't help our confusion about God's love. Many times after the glow of the honeymoon with God fades, we act like Adam and Eve. When we become aware of our sin, instead of running towards our Father in confession, our failure leads us to feel shame, avoid, rationalize and cover up our sin. Like both Adam and Eve, we hide from God.

I can never remember not believing in God and not having a relationship with Jesus, even when it was deciding I didn't like Him. Yet, because my understanding of Him carried so much distortion, my life in Him was lived in self-deception.

God – as I imagined Him – along with my struggle to please Him, I saw as signs of a healthy and close relationship. I even thought of it as an intimate relationship. It was not. It lacked the comfort, peace and closeness God means us to feel in His company. I felt good around Him as long as I thought I was doing well. Believe me that was hit or miss, mostly miss, when perfection is the standard.

I didn't understand there is peace between us. Peace is His gift to each of us. When we think of the word peace in English, we think

of tranquility or an absence of strife... but the Bible wasn't written in English! What the Hebrew word peace (Shalom) means is:
to be whole, without deficiency. The other meaning of the word
we translate peace means to be at unity. When we join these two
meanings it makes a world of difference. Before Him I am whole,
I have no deficiencies in Christ Jesus. When we put our faith in
Jesus and are born again, we are a new creation in Him. We become one with Christ. This means my failures are not based in my
deficiencies and lack of perfection, they are based in my immaturity as a new creation in Christ. That is a completely different
paradigm. I am a perfectly normal and whole immature person.
As a parent, I do not hold against my children the fact that they
are not where they one day will be. To get to maturity, you have
to grow, walk, stumble, and fall through immaturity. That means
failures, lots of them. It means dealing with selfishness, fear, un-
belief and ignorance. God as our parent, and our creator who is
perfect, loves us as we are. He doesn't look at us with an angry
face and an upraised arm. He doesn't give us the silent treatment
and isolate us as punishment. His expectation is immaturity. He
adores us and is wisely helping us towards maturity. That is a
lifelong process of taking off the old to put on the new. It is not always pleasant. It will culminate when "the last trumpet is blown
and we will all be changed in the blink of an eye" (1 Cor. 15:52).
In the meantime God is delighted to be at one with us. In Christ,
there is not just peace between us, but a oneness and unity. We are
in Christ, He is in God, God is in Him and we are in God.

What freedom there is when you do not feel you have to avoid
God because of failure. I may come sad, glad, confused, angry or
full of gratitude, but I am free in His presence, be it when I am falling on my face in repentance or dancing on my toes in victory.

I can say anything and not feel ashamed. I bring my failures,
my joys and my questions to Him. I listen for and welcome His
perspective. God does not always answer me in the way I expect,
nor according to my time schedule. God does correct when it is

needed. At times that isn't a painless experience – but I liken it to a healthy maturity adjustment so that I might grow and become wiser. If we all thought of God's correction as "maturity adjustments," it would help us to not be as fearful of correction, viewing it rightly. Can some failures be sin? Absolutely! It is always a sin to steal! And what God says to us about sin, is bring it out of the dark by confessing it in the assurance that I (God) am just and will forgive that sin and cleanse you (1 Jn. 1:9). The justice of your forgiveness is this: Jesus paid that sin's penalty on the Cross.

I go to a chiropractor regularly. There is a sheath over a muscle in my leg that sometimes tightens. When it does it causes my foot to turn outward, which affects my balance. When this happens the chiropractor runs pressure down the sheath in order to loosen it. That adjustment causes enough pain that I cannot help but groan out loud. Afterwards the pain disappears and I am amazed at the result in my body. What was wrong is made right and my balance is restored. If we get stuck in immaturity our entire gait with God and others is distorted. God knows when we need adjusting – usually there is some pain involved – sometimes so much that we groan out loud. But it is good: the pain passes, and in the end it restores our balance.

Job, (there is a book in the Old Testament of the Bible named after him), gets a most lengthy "maturity adjustment" when he questions God, demanding an answer because he feels innocent and wronged by Him. God "adjusts his thinking," by asking Job a series of questions that are quite painful. They begin with, "Who are you to question my wisdom? Where were you when I laid the foundations of the earth? Who determined its dimensions and stretched out the surveying line? What supports its foundations, and who laid its cornerstone as the morning stars sang together and all the angels shouted for joy?!" (Job 38:2-7). God goes on to adjust Job's thinking and attitude for four more chapters. We know this conversation was not motivated by God's anger because of where the story ends. God had a deep love for Job –

even in His silence at Job's sufferings. Job fully repents of his folly. Instead of God shaming him, He restores all Job lost. In fact God doubles his lost fortune and then doubles the blessings in the second half of his life. He extends his life an additional 140 years (4 generations of children and grandchildren to be enjoyed; Job 42:10-17).

There is always more to be discovered in God! He loves me completely. Like Job, I have not yet discovered all the pride that is within me. Like Job, I do not understand God. And like Job, when I share my all (the good, bad and ugly) with God and He honors me by sharing his greater perspectives, the wonder of our love goes deeper. I am the one whose life expands.

When Job comes to the end of his "adjustment" this is what he says: "Now I know you can do anything and no one can stop you.... I was talking about things I knew nothing about, things far too wonderful for me.... I had only heard about you before, now I have seen you with my own eyes" (Job 42:2, 3, 5). This *can be* the fruit of correction. It is certainty the intended purpose of God. I am glad that God is patient when I am speaking about things I know nothing about. In fact, I think I sometimes feel His smile embrace my immaturity.

That isn't the only place we sometimes find a cancer of wrong thinking plaguing our peace in God. When I was a child I heard a thousand times when I was wanting to set out on some new adventure, "you must ask permission first." While I am not advocating permissive parenting that allows children to jump off a cliff should they want to, not all risks should be avoided. Success was my parent's ultimate goal. Inconvenience or embarrassment was to be avoided. Adventures were approved or rejected based on this criteria rather than perceived as an opportunity to expand my experiences of life. They didn't seem to understand that both success and failure are great teachers, nor that failure is often the better teacher. They also didn't understand that failure was not a reflection of my worth or my level of intelligence. Instead, for them failure carried the greatest of negative consequences. I could not fail and receive either my parent's approval or blessing. Rather than living in their approval I had to bear the burden of their rejection and ridicule. Instead of being at peace, I was always anxious. They believed this to be the greater teacher.

I know God is not like this. My experience is that He is the God of permission (not to sin, of course). We can fail a thousand times and not be shy about drawing close to His love. We need not fear His reprimand. In the book of Acts when the Gentiles come to faith and Peter is telling the apostles and other believers in Jerusalem about this, they responded by praising God and saying, "we can see that God has also given the Gentiles the privilege of repenting of their sins and receiving eternal life" (Acts 11:18). In other words they have the privilege of being welcomed before God and receiving His favor – in the midst of failure.

We all waste plenty of God's money and our own time and passion taking risks that don't work out as we'd imagined. I sometimes think God is crazy to continue to entrust us with his riches... Yet I sense His joy in risk takers. The greater the risk, the greater the potential fruit, and the greater the faith or foolishness required. This is a wonderful thing.

I know He loves who we are. He loves our essence. Speaking personally I know He loves my imagination and my creativity. I know he loves that it's married to a need to be practical. I know He isn't comparing me to anyone else.

It is the same for you. He loves who you are, in all your complexities. He isn't comparing you to anyone else. This is the person He encourages to take risks. If it's any help to you, I often take comfort in the meaning of the word risk: there is some good possibility of failure! God is not just aware of this, He is behind it.

I do not love failing, I don't know anyone who does! I consider the odds of failure before engaging in a project or relationship, counting the cost of failure. I also pray a lot before taking a risk! What is true is that when I have given it my best shot, I am rarely ashamed of failing. It does not rob me of peace with God. It doesn't wiggle its way into other areas of my mind and torment me. I don't spend much time at all in self-criticism or ridicule. Failure is a great Holy Spirit empowered teacher if you'll take its lessons to heart. Unless you embrace failure in this way, it can steal your peace.

There is another peace robber. The issue of our control! It doesn't go well with Godly peace, even though we often do feel peace with God when we feel in control. Yet it's a shaky peace at best, because it is rooted in us not God. The true benefits of peace in God come in letting Him lead – even when we do not know the short term destination. I frequently say: "God is the one who keeps lots of cards up His sleeve. Draw near to Him and you have absolutely no idea what the map of your life will look like." Not all roads are ones you'd have chosen for yourself. I still remind myself that an adventure isn't an adventure unless there is a measure of the unknown and lots of things I will not be able to control.

One of my more memorable experiences with God's secret cards was when I was helping out in Teen Ministry. I was looking for a vehicle by which teenagers could reach out to our community in fun ways they would enjoy while allowing them to share the love of Jesus. We had a professional clown in our church who was an expert at balloon sculptures. I invited her to come and give lessons on making balloon animals and sculptures to our teens. Of course the teens and I learned together. We had a totally wonderful time of laughter in the learning. This led to some great outreaches the teens did in malls and grocery stores, parks and events. Soon there were stories of God encounters. I began getting calls from churches asking me to come and teach balloon making. I would take teens to help out. I shall never forget watching one of our teens teach a blind woman how to make a balloon animal as I fought back tears. I found myself teaching balloon making to people of all ages around New England. Then I found myself teaching balloon making in Spain. Christians in another country were using this little tool to reach out to people in their parks.

ARE YOU KIDDING ME! I never ever would have imagined this to be something I would do. I am a serious Bible teacher, a pastor, and counselor. It was so unlike me as to make me unrecognizable to close friends. It was a card God dealt me that resulted in an explosion of joy. It came from letting God be in control. That season was not my plan. It was out of my box. Isn't that just God? We often stumble into things that change our lives when we are willing to give up control and follow a path not of our making.

The Lord of Heavens Armies is not fighting against us – He is fighting for us. It looks very different than what we'd imagined. Not all of God's cards lead us to such short term joy. There are the Aces and Kings and then there are the Jokers. These peace stealer sometimes include our misunderstanding his "No's." We often assign negative motives to our Father when he says no.

When God says "no" it is said in peace. He says hard things in ways that are often filled with encouragement. When He says "no" to one of my ideas or requests, or points out thinking that is off base, while I am often disappointed, He says it in ways that don't cause me to feel pushed away. I have often thought about the passage where He tells King David no. David is about to do a very wonderful thing for God from a pure heart of love… but God says "uh-uh-no, David, you are a bit off base…"

> David summoned all the officials of Israel to Jerusalem – the leaders of the tribes, the commanders of the army divisions, the other generals and the captains, the overseers of the royal property and livestock, the palace officials, the mighty men, and all the other brave warriors in the kingdom. David rose to his feet and said: "My brothers and my people! It was my desire to build a temple where the Ark of the Lord's Covenant, God's

footstool, could rest permanently. I made necessary preparations for building it, but God said to me, 'You must not build a temple to honor my name, for you are a warrior and have shed much blood.' Yet the Lord, the God of Israel, has chosen me from among all my father's family to be King over Israel forever. For he has chosen the tribe of Judah to rule, and from among the families of Judah, he chose my father's family. And from among my father's sons the Lord was pleased to make me King over all Israel. And from among my sons – for the Lord has given me many – he chose Solomon to succeed me on the throne of Israel to rule over the Lord's Kingdom.... And he said to me, 'Your son Solomon will build my temple and its courtyards, I have chosen him to be my son and I will be his father...'"

I Chronicles 28: 1-7

David reports to his most trusted leaders the conversation in which God tells him he is disqualified to build the temple because he is "a man of war and has shed much blood!" Yet who was it that led David to war on behalf of the kingdom? It was God. The very thing David was called by God to do – an act of obedience – disqualified him from his desire to honor God by building Him a house. Yet there is no resentment detected in David's voice. There is no bitterness communicated to his leaders as he told them of this "NO" from God. David is a man under authority who has heard many no's and experienced the blessing, provision and protection that follow in the wake of God's wisdom. He knows God is not pushing him away. He is doing something much wiser than David would have ever chosen on his own.

God's no's are doorways that lead to unexplored hallways that are far better than we could ever have imagined. A no is sometimes excruciatingly painful, but trusting that there is a promise of a better way is incredibly comforting. I've seen the better again and again. I am living right now in the wake of such a "no." I was able to let go of my dream, one God granted us for a season, and carry on in gratitude. I am in disbelief of what has resulted four years later. Both my husband and I sometimes pinch ourselves and say: "Is this blessing really ours?" It would have never been possible had we not embraced a NO, not knowing what was ahead…

It is not easy to let God be in control – particularly when it involves a crossroad experience. These are some of the hardest no's of all. We can feel deeply hurt or abandoned by God. Life was one way and headed one direction, then suddenly there is a sign with a very different and unknown destination. A place we have no desire to travel to. Our peace with God evaporates. We are deeply hurt by the discrepancy between His plans and ours. The lack of peace is not on His side. He understands the road to the cross better than we do. There is a much deeper peace He gives when we trust His leadership in no's. Often this trust is something we have to fight to give Him; and we travel through some turbulent waters along the way. The waves can be so high we cannot see above them, and we feel no assurance they will end. We can feel the victim of a cruel joke. To trust God is an act of blind obedience. We don't always see the blessing in this life time, but God's no's always have blessing attached. His wisdom always leads to more life. He is always fighting for us.

I am graven on the palms of his hands.
I am never out of His mind.
All my knowledge of Him depends on his
sustained initiative in knowing me.
He knows me as a friend.
One who loves me, and there is no moment
when His eye is off me, or his attention is distracted
from me, and no moment therefore, when his care falters.

J. I. PACKER

4

LOVE COMES SOFTLY

A surprise by nature is something we are not expecting. There are good surprises and painful ones. Not all surprises come from God! And He doesn't deliver them via an embossed envelope with a beautifully scripted announcement enclosed. Nor does it come by a messenger who proclaims it by raising a trumpet to his mouth. Usually surprises sneak up on us. This is also true of coming to understand God's great love. We have spectacular moments of experiencing it, but understanding that love is different. For most all of us this tends to be more like an unfolding. Love is very complex under the best of circumstances.

We are trained from a very early age to believe that good performance equals approval and reward. (I used chocolate kisses and high praise to reward my children for using the potty. I made certain they knew I approved of their changed behavior.)

By the time we reach school age, every day that message is reinforced when we turn in a homework paper or test and receive a letter grade. The goal of course is to get A's on our report card. If you get A's then you get additional recognition and honor by everyone from parents to the school administration. Participation in sports is the same: the children who are most gifted get the cheers, the ones less so, the boo's. I was terrible at sports. When it would be my turn to hit in softball, or serve in volleyball, everyone on the opposing team would begin to chant: "Easy Out, Easy Out." I felt ashamed even before I was up, because it was true. I knew what was coming. I was an "easy out." I was going to let my team down. They always put me last so they could mitigate, as much as possible, having me assigned to the team. This was repeated in most every area of my life.

Our brains are as amazing as they are complex. Putting it in simple terms (and it isn't simple), when we have an experience repeatedly, we develop a pathway of thought in our brain. I once had a counselor explain it as a road on which our thoughts naturally travel. I think the image she used is helpful. The more experiences we receive that confirm the message, the more entrenched that road becomes. In fact it becomes a major highway.

Our bodies have a natural style of conserving energy. By conserving in one area it becomes available in another. Well-rehearsed patterns allow our thoughts to jump on the existing highway all by themselves. When I head out to work, I take a right out of the driveway, a right at the end of the street, go straight for some distance, then take a left just after the stop light at the street our church is on, then I take a left into the driveway. I don't think about it, in fact, I don't even notice it unless there is a problem with traffic or weather. Even then, I am not focused on the route, I am negotiating the challenge. I do this automatically. This is how we get along in life. It is a great design. It allow us to maximize our energy and build upon knowledge we have already stored up. At times it can also be a hurtful design because sometimes the road we travel is full of potholes. Life is more complicated than what was presented to us as children. This is particularly true when it comes to performance, approval, value and reward. They are enmeshed in our understanding of love.

God designed our brains, so this doesn't take Him by surprise. He isn't angered by the highways of thought that are not helpful. Instead He is in the reconstruction business. That is an important thing to remember about God. For us to think differently about something we've been trained in, it means a new roadway of thought has to be created.

The reality that we are loved because God is love and passionately loves us – regardless of performance – requires a new roadway of thinking to be created. We need God to re-orient our brains.

Most of our paths of thought initiate from the great "I" as the starting point. I am the center. Mommy wants ME to use the potty so she rewards ME with praise and candy. God's roadways start with God. He is the center. Stay with me....

When we begin to believe in God, our thoughts about Him jump on the highway that is already laid in our minds. They usually tell us good performance equals approval, value and reward. As long as "I" am doing what "I" perceive is good, "I" stay close to God. When "I" believe I'm doing poorly, "I" withdraw and either get angry, or work to jump through hoops of my own imagining. For some period of time "I" feel appropriate, "I" punish myself or work to improve myself, to prove to God "I" am doing well again because "I" think this makes Him feel better about me. Then emotionally "I" feel good and call that restoration. Can you see that this is a roadway of thought whose starting point is I?

That is not God's definition of restoration. Our restoration to right relationship with God is because He is the starting point. God himself loves us already. He is pursuing us. He sent His Son to do what we cannot do! As a perfect man He took our imperfections on Himself at the cross. He carried them to the tomb. I don't know what those days in the tomb hidden from human sight looked like. What we do know is that after three days God raised Him from the dead – and that was the proof that we were forgiven. Forgiveness isn't earned; it's accepted. When we put our faith in Jesus and follow Him, the work of the cross is complete in our lives. We can't live unblemished lives. That is not our Father's expectation. We are forgiven because we ALREADY have His favor. He is the starting point.

Our behavior is important to God, but it is NOT a means to gain His love and acceptance. That is already secure. Were this not true, the thief on the cross next to Jesus could not have been accepted into the kingdom. But we know he was accepted because he already had a place of favor in God's heart. His only act on earth was to believe in Jesus and admit his wrong. He accepted God's favor.

Behavior is an amazingly practical tool. Like a mirror it reflects what is in our heart. Whenever I over-react to something, I immediately know something is amiss inside of me. Behavior is a means of honoring God – of making oneself available to Him. It's allowing us to work in partnership with Him. We are the demonstration of the reality of His personhood, Kingdom, power, love, and plan, to both the seen and unseen world around us.

We will always need to deal with sin. It is going to be with us in measure until we die. 1 John 1:8-9 says, "If we claim we have no sin, we are only fooling ourselves and not living in the truth. But if we confess our sins to Him, He is faithful and just to forgive us our sins and to cleanse us from all wickedness." Confession, repentance, receiving forgiveness and God's cleansing are the only means of dealing with our impure hearts. It's not something we do one time – we do it over and over for as long as it takes to see that sin destroyed and that area healed of its weakness.

Unless you know this in your knower – that God draws near to the humble and weak – you will not be able to relax in His presence. You won't be able to truly enjoy His presence, or the strengthening of His direction. His presence has words of enlightening insight and healing. You won't easily recognize His voice. In seasons when you are functioning in failure, instead of running towards Him for His love and help, you will avoid Him at all cost, insulating yourself from the pain of what you believe will be His displeasure and rejection. All of this is the result of a highway of thought that equates failure to punishment and rejection, and good performance to approval, value and reward (love).

God sees differently. He looks not at the outward performance/appearance, but at the inward heart. Motive not outcome is what God measures. He doesn't measure it to smack us, rather to give us praise. It is very hard for us to see inside our own hearts!

In the Bible, Paul says he doesn't evaluate his own heart because he would not be a good judge of his own motives. He tells us not to judge ourselves or others before the Lord returns – for only He can see our darkest secrets and our inner motives (I Cor. 4:5). Paul ends this verse by saying, "Then God will give to each one whatever praise is due." He does not say, then He will give to each what punishment is due. This tells me that what God looks for in each of His children is a reason to genuinely praise. And the praise He gives is based on our inner secrets and motives. This is a game changer. It devalues performance to its proper place. It is a mere shadow or a reflection of a "secret" that only God knows.

There are so many factors and outcomes that are not in our control. We live in a world of interdependence where none of us is an island. We live in different countries with varying degrees of freedom and provision. Illness is in the mix. There is the presence of evil. There are so many circumstances and environments in which it makes no difference how well you perform – you are not going to succeed at attaining a desired outcome. If you were to either judge yourself or be judged by others, it would appear you'd failed.

Our highways of thought must start with who God is. He loves at all times. God can and wants to lay down new highways of thought in our minds. I mentioned that I had an experience that began changing my perspective of how God sees life through such different lenses than us. I am going to review it again to refresh your memory, and then share how God used it to begin helping me to see as He sees.

I mentioned as a young girl I had a very developed love for and sense of God's presence. I sought to please Him in all I did. My mom was a strong willed woman with many broken areas in her own life. I am sure I inherited my own strong will from her. Part of her brokenness was to believe she was correct in her evaluation of every incident in life. If she believed you to be guilty, you were guilty. One of her pet peeves was being lied to (which drives all parents crazy). She couldn't tolerate lying. It was the ultimate insult and act of disrespect. My own developing strong will needed to please God above all else. At times it was in conflict with her version of truth and a war of wills would result. It is not easy to think of a little girl fighting for truth against a grown woman who was committed to preserving her authority and version of truth. She was sure her actions were preventing a child liar from becoming an adult liar. It is not easy for me to share this part of our history, yet it is so profoundly central to my coming to understand the love of God that I cannot leave it unspoken.

Because of the pain inflicted I never won those wars with my mother. We were both fighting for the same thing: truth. In the end I would lie by agreeing with my mother to stop the pain and preserve my life. Each and every time the physical pain would be replaced with days of emotional pain at letting God down by lying to save my own skin. I would sincerely repent and promise that the next time this happened I would not give in. I would not lie. But I never was able to keep my promise. I was as sincere in my promise as Peter was to Jesus when he promised he would never deny Him. And like Peter, I was just as wrong at judging my own strength of character. That failure I carried with me for years.

I made it through childhood – left home at 18 and married a wonderful man. Together we began to serve God. Twelve years later I was with him in Jerusalem. We had taken a tour with others from our church. Derek Prince was tagging along with us from time to time. We'd arrived and had gotten settled into our rooms at the hotel. It was the beginning of the Jewish Sabbath. We were exhausted after the very long flight and so taking a rest on our bed. It was a warm evening and the windows that swung open to our small veranda allowed a lovely breeze to refresh us. We could hear the men in the synagogue below begin a song of worship. As we listened suddenly a young child who was in a house not far from us began to sing. His voice was so sweet and crystal clear as he sang the same Sabbath songs the men below sang. If ever I could have been frozen in time, to this day I would have chosen that moment. As I lay there on my bed listening to this child worship – in disbelief I was in Jerusalem – I began to pray with tears of gratitude. I said, "God how did I get here – I grew up poor – from nowhere – my parents divorced – I did poorly in school – I am not educated – my childhood was terrible. Yet I am married to a wonderful man who loves me and loves you deeply. I have traveled to visited several different countries, been a missionary in Africa, have 4 amazing children. I have in-laws that love me as if I was their own daughter, we are leaders in our church and now I am here in Jerusalem. How did this happen?" As clearly as I have heard anything in my life, God answered me in a most unexpected way.

> "Do you remember the beatings you took as a child for truth?
> I saw every one. I was with you.
> What you counted as failure – I counted as success."

It had been more than 20 years since that season in my childhood. God, my Father took me half way around the world to the land Jesus walked, on the Sabbath – the time for appointed rest – to a hotel room close to another child who was worshipping God in isolation. There He let me know He was present with me all those years ago. He had witnessed what I thought was my failure. He let me know He hadn't forgotten it nor seen it the same way. He had treasured what I had seen as a failure. He had seen it as an act of pure worship. Not because of my perfect performance, but because of my heart.

I was undone – that wound in my heart was healed. Love had come softly. A new highway of thought gently began to be laid in my mind.

Intimacy with God is what determines our exploits.

SUNDAY ADELAJA

5

INTIMACY WITH GOD

Intimacy – a word that is loaded with emotion. From anyone's perspective it has to be part of a lifestyle of loving God. Depending on your background, predisposition, and experience, the word can mean many different things. I don't mean it in a touchy feely kind of way nor in a religious way. I don't mean it in a highly emotional way, which leads some to develop erratic patterns of living. They consider themselves tuned into the "Voice of God." And God keeps them turning on a dime. I am also not referring to some mystical connection to God. For me the mystical is just that – mystical. I find it complicated, impractical, and uncomfortable.

There are no right or wrong personality types – each is made by God. It's His gift to us and we do well to function within our natural style. Every book you find on growing a lifestyle of intimacy with God will reflect the personality and style of the author.

I think it is important to note that different approaches are not right or wrong. Each will resonate with a particular type of person. When you find an approach that fits you, it isn't because it is better than others – it's because it's a match for who you are.

I am artistic, have a teaching gift, and I carry a prophetic anointing. These gifts are married to a driving desire for the practical. If things aren't practical to everyday people, I have little use for them. I am not saying that is ideal, just that it reflects me. Therefore it is the accent with which I speak about intimacy.

Have you read the story of the boy David, fighting the giant Goliath in the Bible (1 Samuel 17:32-50)? David is offered the armor of the King for a fight with Goliath. As he tries it on, he found that it was in fact a hindrance. David needed the stripped down version of himself and a simple slingshot, the weapon he was practiced in. He knew his true weapon was a person who fought next to him: God! Although unseen, He was bigger and more real than any insulting giant. It was in being true to who he was that David declares his intimate connection to the Lord of Heaven's Armies! Goliath didn't stand a chance.

Simply put, intimacy with God means a heart connection that is closer than a friend. A bond in the deepest and healthiest sense of the word. Like family, only even more so, God knows you at your best and worst and has a stake in the outcome of the relationship.

This is not true of friends. I have had treasured and intimate friends change their mind about our relationship. My experience is that friends come and go as people, interests, and needs change.

The type of intimate connection I am suggesting that is possible with God is intimacy more like that of twins. They are buck naked in the same womb from the time they are 2 separate cells. They are different people, but connection from inception creates a different bond than normal siblings. God our creator, who is perfect and the God of the universe, has always and forever been right next to us. The Bible says He knew us before we were born.

We can't keep anything from Him. It is a tie that time, distance, and experience cannot break. Love, trust, and loyalty, without fear of violation, would most describe the characteristics of an intimate relationship with God.

David had this type of relationship with King Saul's son, Jonathan. Jonathan made a solemn pact with David because he loved him as he loved himself (I Sam. 18:3). David also had this type of intimacy with God, not so much because of David's deep and great love for God, which he demonstrated multiple times, but because God loved David as He loved Himself! God described him as "David, a man after my own heart" (I Sam. 13:14, Acts 13:22). God would just not let David go, even when David proved unfaithful to that same unity of heart (2 Sam. 12:13-14).

Let's explore some of the sides of intimacy we don't often consider. It's hard work that doesn't come naturally or often easily. It's risky.

I have been married to my husband for over 50 years. Ours is a relationship marked by intimacy. I was 18 and he was 22 when we married. Anyone who has a healthy relationship with their spouse and has been married for any length of time will tell you it involves up, down, good, hard, unexciting, exciting, devastating, blessed, disappointing, angry, unspeakable joy-filled, unexpected, and unpredictable times. In fact, intimacy is best formed out of persevering in hard times of resolving conflict, rather than simply sharing good times together. It is being together in suffering that drives you to reach for deeper intimacy and more meaningful relationship.

Our relationship has required lots of hard work by both of us. It's meant taking intimacy risks that scare the heebie-jeebies out of you. (He/she may blow up or walk away when I tell him/her this.)

What we have now is different than what we started with. In the beginning of the relationship I was madly in love with Don, but I was not always truthful. Now, there is nothing I can't tell him –

the good, the bad, the ugly, the dreams, the fears, the sins. I can still surprise him, but then I guess that's because I still surprise myself. I can almost never shock him. He has been a white board upon which I can explore my innermost thoughts and emotions without the fear of being judged. Instead of judgment I have received understanding and encouragement. He has **access** to my heart and emotions.

Access would describe one side of intimacy.

Without access our relationship of love would be shallow. I can hear things from Don that I can't hear from others. He has the ability to help me adjust my attitudes, to view something from a different perspective, to point out when I am being self-centered, deceived, too hard on myself or someone else. He challenges me to new horizons and asks questions that cause me to evaluate the things I am accountable for. In other words, he has **access** not just to my heart and emotions but to my mind. He helps me think and review the decisions I am making, and he does it in a non-judgmental way. He has **access** to the whole of me, and I to him. This is God's goal in marriage: "the two shall become one flesh and they were naked and not ashamed." *The sexual act is simply a physical sign of the reality of two people willingly being fully joined spiritually. It was created as a means of pleasure out of which something totally new is born.*

Intimacy with the God of the Universe isn't sexual, it is spiritual. It is an act of bringing all of who you are to Jesus in order to be fully known and to know. It is transparent (naked) communication, meant to include your heart, emotions, your thoughts, dreams and fears. It expects to be heard, but also wants to hear and be impacted by the other's perspective. (I see Don as one who, though different than me, enriches my limited views.) In marriage it means times where I am present for an extended period of time every day for this depth of conversation to take place. It is the same with God, I have to be present to Him physically and emotionally for intimacy to be forged. (We come boldly before the throne of grace.) This is something meant to be looked forward to, not avoided or run from. Out of it, new things will be born.

I am emphasizing access as a significant key to growing intimacy. Access is something we give to another of our own free will. If it is acquired by any other means, it is an act of abuse or invasion. It will not produce intimacy. God will not force you into an intimate relationship with Him. He gives access, an invitation, and His favor.

Each of us has a door of access to our heart/life. It is part of being human. It is latched on our side and we guard that latch. We are the one with the power and authority to unlock it. I have granted Don access to the depths of who I am because of his demonstrated love towards me. He has proven himself faithful and trustworthy. It is the same with God. The degree of access we give God, is the depth of intimacy that results. The degree to which we trust God will affect the level of access we give him.

Can one demonstrate love, but have that love misunderstood? Yes! It happens with people and it happens with God. He faithfully demonstrates His love; but it doesn't always get through. This has to do with what we believe about God in the first place.

I believe it is a major strategy of the devil to attack the goodness of God. He wants us to doubt our standing in God, to distort our view of His love and authority, to sow seeds of distrust and suspicion in our hearts. It is a strategy that is effective and it dates back to the Garden of Eden. It works as well with men as it does with women.

When Don and I were much younger, he scheduled a very costly surprise for my birthday. He had registered us for a marriage conference on my birthday weekend. The day before my birthday he announced his costly gift of love. I was furious. I had younger children, we didn't have much money, and time off was very precious. I didn't want to spend my birthday or our preciously small resources sitting in meetings with a bunch of people I didn't know.

On top of that, when he announced his gift, I believed he was trying to tell me he was dissatisfied with me and our marriage without hurting my feelings by telling me this directly. I'd assigned a motive that simply was not in his heart. His demonstrated gift of love was completely misunderstood and led to my becoming angry. We worked it through, which was pretty painful. It meant tears of repentance on my part and forgiveness on his part. I had hurt his feelings by being both ungrateful and accusatory.

It turned out Don wasn't dissatisfied with our relationship, he highly valued it. And he wasn't dissatisfied with me. He thought I would be totally blessed by spending dedicated time just with him, talking about and enjoying us! I had wrongly believed something that simply was not in his heart. I was behaving towards him according to my fantasy of what he was thinking. His love "didn't get through" my veil of misunderstanding.

I did this to God for years. It was why I tormented myself as a child – believing I had failed God when I would give in to my mom and lie to stop a beating. It was why I was so thankful I'd done the ceremony called baptism that allowed God to accept me. It was why I always needed to perform well to feel God's love.

Our false beliefs about God are rooted in our experience of demonstrated love, primarily through our parents and other significant authority figures in our life. We can't help it. God doesn't hold it against us. He understands our history far better than we do.

I recently heard someone pray, "God I thank you so much that you love us in spite of who we are." I think what he meant was: "I know you love us in the midst of our being sinners." This is perfectly true. The thought, however, that God loves us in spite of who we are places an emphasis on our fallen nature, rather than on God loving us because of WHO we are. We are His precious and beloved children. It can feed into an understanding of God that fuels our sense of unworthiness and frames Him as a judge. I was recently counseling a young woman who was quite angry at God. After listening for a long time, I said to her: "I think your problem is rooted in the fact that you are not yet convinced that God is truly good." After several moments of silent reflection, she said, "You are right. I see him more like a lawyer. If you do this list of things, then I will bless you." Then she said, "I really think if I haven't prayed for my daughter's safety at night, God will not keep her safe." Many of us would be shocked by her response, but in my experience, many would believe the same about God. It would just be in a different area. I am convinced we don't appreciate how much God loves us.

Just for a moment consider how God sees us. When His eyes are upon us, He sees so much more than the moment we are living right now. He sees the whole of our lives. That began even before our birth. I had one son who was born with a blister on his top lip from sucking his thumb in the womb. Before he was born he was already in the habit of self-comforting. God knows that about him. As his mother, it was an endearing quality. We have many endearing qualities to God. He knows our childhood, the struggles we may have fought to overcome in school. He knows the brave face we put on when our best friend moved, the torment we went through because of being terrified of the dark, or the teacher who mistreated us. He understands why you closed down emotionally when your father left. He sees the damage done by staying in six foster homes by the time you were three years old. He knows you grew up in a privileged home where you were spoiled by things but had little access to your parents' time. He saw that you were not the favorite child. He understands the shame you suffered because you weren't a good enough student, athlete, musician, were overweight or too skinny. He knows the burden of feeling ugly, of not being able to measure up to the expectation of another.

Our stories go on and on. We are not a moment in time, we are a book that includes our past and a future not yet lived. God sees us very clearly from beginning to end. He sees outside of time, and He sees from the perspective of a loving Father. He is tenderhearted. He has been with you every day. The Bible tells us that every day of our life has been recorded in His book (Psalm 139:16). It could not have been recorded had He not been there ahead of you. His vision sets things in a larger context. It includes the hardness of life in a world where sin is present.

He often thinks much more highly of us than we think of ourselves. He loves us not in spite of ourselves, but because He knows us and treasures our spunk and resilience. Jesus lived our life. He understands we can't be perfect. Because of the great love God has for us, Jesus died in our place to secure that His Father's love would get through!

God is kind towards us. If you think of God as a judging Father with very high expectations, suspend that thought and let this one fill your mind: He has been rooting for you your entire life. He loves you with a pure love. He loves you completely, which means He accepts you as you are right now with all your imperfections. He has demonstrated it over and over and yet we can be blind to it.

Our image of Him defines who we believe Him to be. I was broken-hearted when I awoke to the reality that I had attributed to God motives and a nature He simply was not guilty of. I worshipped a God of my own making. In my version of God, He was not easily entreated nor was He pleased with me most days.

We grant only partial access of heart to those we are afraid of. We protect ourselves, often not even realizing that is what we are doing. It is crazy when I think of it now – for years I honestly and sincerely worshiped and praised God, all the time thinking His greatest priority was trying to make me behave so He could like me better.

I don't pretend to know who God really is. I know more of Him. I know He is totally good, that is my starting point. I also know He is totally other than me. The fact is we can't know or understand anything without comparing it in some way to ourselves. God is not human. His ways are higher, His thoughts are higher...and it's a big higher! In Isaiah 55:9, He tells us the distance between how we think and how He thinks is the distance between heaven and earth. Yet He chooses to make His dwelling with men, to draw us close, to give us access and to bring heaven to earth.

Why would I not want to have Him around all the time? Why wouldn't I want to invite Him to speak to me when I pick blueberries, when I am creating a beautiful necklace, watching a movie, am out shopping, fixing a great meal, or watching a sunset in silence?

Creating a lifestyle of loving God begins with intimacy, which means doing the work of intimacy....

Your father God loves you. You are always at the top of His list. He's happy to take the unreal you because He sees past your pretending. He is longing to meet with the real you, the authentic and unafraid-of-His-presence you. He takes us where we are, even when it includes a confused understanding of who He is. And this is just another thing that makes Him so wonderful, so worthy of praise that it sometimes takes my breath away. I believe in HIS love. I wrap it around myself as I get down to the practical business of bringing His kingdom to the rest of life. That is my heart for us all.

6

BECOMING AUTHENTIC

I'm known as a pretty good cook. I've won several first and second prizes in small cooking contests. I'm not a GREAT cook, but I am better than many and people love eating at our home. I could become a better cook. I am still learning, experimenting, and expanding my experiences in cooking. To become an expert cook would require an investment of time and effort beyond my interest in cooking, so I am content to be a "pretty good cook" while I enjoy watching with admiration GREAT cooks on TV.

When I cook there are several elements I am bringing together. For a good outcome I need fresh ingredients, the right spices, adequate prep time, the correct tools, right proportions, a good source and duration of even heat, and constant tastings. If one of these elements is off, the outcome can be dramatically affected. I personally know the disaster that can occur when everything is perfect, but you use an inexpensive pan, or the heat is too high.

We often don't appreciate what goes into preparing a mouthful of joy. It is the same in loving God. It takes lots of individual elements brought together well to create a lifestyle that runs on His joy-filled presence. It doesn't just happen. If our understanding of the nature of God is wrong, even if we are good at allowing God access to our lives, the result will not be what we had hoped. I have written about our understanding of love, the law of access, misunderstanding the nature of God and how it affects intimacy, the role of behavior and performance. All of these are needed for the recipe.

As we lay hold of health in each of these areas, we experience more consistency, satisfaction, joy, peace, love and power. I have written about the need for transparency and authenticity. They are crucial factors to becoming healthy in every area. But there is more to be said about the roles of these two comrades.

Again using marriage as an example: until each partner knows their spouse genuinely loves them for who they are, and each begins to function in that knowledge, they will not have realized the potential for good in the marriage.

It is the same in Jesus; it is in knowing we are genuinely loved as we are, that we are free to love back. It is in "living in God," – that is in the true love He as for the real us – that His love is made known within us (I John 4:16-17). This is where the potential in partnership with God is realized. It allows full trust and confidence to grow. It is in knowing we are loved that we can relax and get onto the purpose in the partnership. That includes "new creation," but we are not going to go there right now.

This idea of being known poses an important question. If God already fully knows and loves us, why do we need to be transparent to feel His love?

This is such a great question and one I've been asked many times. I think it is helpful to ask a question back. We have all been children. When you were hiding something from your mom or dad, did you FEEL like they totally loved you?

Even if you knew that they knew you were hiding something, you likely didn't feel they loved you. I propose that is because you were not being the real you! You were pretending you were someone else, usually an innocent you! You clothed yourself in a costume, and that costume was a lie for the purpose of deception and protection. Deception of who you were and protection from who you believed them to be. It also was self-protection from how you believed they would respond. When we are in costume, love is sabotaged. It feels deceptive because love requires transparency and truth to be genuine.

We need to be transparent and authentic with God because unless the real me is the person I know He loves, it feels like love is a game, an illusion of my making. It cuts me off from experiencing God's love.

Of course, this is not true. God is big enough to work with the real you at the same time He is working with the pretend you. We are the ones who can't handle our own deception. This becomes a seriously limiting factor to intimate relationship with Him. At least that is my experience. But God doesn't give up. He has a way of patiently walking through the pretend you to get to the real you.

In marriage, God gives us a picture of what relationship with Him is most like. In no other relationship is there a covenant of permanence attached to full exposure without shame. Yet in marriage authenticity happens in stages. My husband describes it in counseling as the "dance of seven veils." There is a progressive unveiling of who we are that tests how genuine the love of the other is. It is typical to discover a spouse has not revealed everything about themselves to the partner before they married. In fact, in some marriages there are events that can remain unmentioned for years because of the frailty of the relationship and fear of shame or rejection.

We do this with God too. As we grow in feeling fully accepted in Him we expose more and more of ourselves before Him. The difference is God does know it all: He sees beneath every veil. He is not going to reject us. Nor is He going to shame us. His love is not only genuine and accepting, it is enduring. It is not going anywhere because it is based on the reality of WHO He is. He fully knows and loves who you are. Paul says in Romans 9:38-39, "I am convinced that nothing can ever separate us from God's love. Neither death nor life, neither angels or demons, neither our fears for today nor our worries about tomorrow – not even powers of hell can separate us from God's love. No power in the sky above or in the earth below is able to separate us from the love of God that is revealed in Christ Jesus our Lord."

If by faith you will start here, you will save yourself years and years of pretending. Be the real, authentic you. That is the one God died for. He did it because of who He is, fully knowing who we are. He did it while we were in the midst of doing destructive stuff and going our own way. Believe me His love can more than adequately handle the real you.

God accepts that we get tired, frustrated, hateful, confused, angry, proud, jealous, and greedy. He accepts that we lie, have disgusting patterns of self-comfort, are fearful and every other negative behavior common to man. Instead of pretending you are other than that – tell Him about it as it displays itself in your life. (The Bible calls it confession.)

You will discover that He doesn't run the other direction, doesn't rebuke, but instead delights to give His help. He delights to kindly take us by the hand and lead us to change. Sometimes it is very hard; but it is such a good hurt.

Let me tell you a story from my own life. I was 18 when my husband and I married. We immediately went to Africa to serve as missionaries. To this day we call it our two-year honeymoon. When we had been there about ten months, Don was called to go to a university outreach several hours away. I couldn't go because he was to stay in a men's dorm. We were apart for several weeks. I was bored and lonely and missed our weekly trips to a dance club. I had the daughter of one of the other missionaries on our team come and stay with me for a weekend. She was 15. Knowing Don and I loved to dance, her mom agreed to let her stay with me if I promised NOT to take her to the dance club. Of course that is all this 15 year old wanted to do. She began begging me to take her the moment she arrived for her weekend stay. Truth be known I wanted to go too, but would never go on my own. On the condition that she not tell her mom, I took her.

Somehow her mom found out, and she confronted me. I looked her straight in the eyes and told her I had no idea why her daughter would have said such a thing. I did not take her to the club. I thought that would be the end of it. To make a long story shorter – I repeatedly stuck to my story over several confrontations that worked their way right up to the head of the missionary organization. When Don came home I stuck to my story and my husband believed me. I was miserable feeling the weight of my lie and feeling cut off from God.

One night several weeks later at a "spiritual retreat" I could no longer stand myself. Don and I were sleeping in bunk beds. I began to silently cry. It caused the bed above to shake. From the top bunk, Don asked what was wrong. I told him I had lied. He had no idea what I was talking about and replied, "You lied about what?" I said "I lied about the club. I took Wendy to the club." He swung himself down from the top bunk and I expected him to be extremely angry. I'd imagined that most terrible conversation a thousand times. Instead he climbed in bed next to me, put his arm around me, pulled me close and told me how much he loved me. Then he said he was disappointed that I'd lied, but that the next day we would go together and I could tell the director and others what I had done. Then he told me not to worry, God was changing me and he stayed with me in that crowded small bed all night.

That night I experienced a different side of my husband's love. And I experienced who my heavenly Father actually was. His love was not ashamed of me. It pulled me close and waited with me through the night. Then he unashamedly went with me to make things right still claiming me as his own. My husband's love was not a natural love. Who cannot be changed by such love? Who cannot trust more deeply, love more fully as a result? That love was part of making me a "new creation." Lying, which had played a big role in my life, was broken. Love broke it in a thousand pieces. Never did it again sit as a throne of protection in my heart. I had been made new by the love of God given through my husband.

"Since we have a great High Priest who has entered heaven, Jesus the Son of God, let us hold firmly to what we believe. This high Priest of ours understands our weaknesses, for He faced all the same testing we do, yet He did not sin. So let us come boldly to the throne of our gracious God. There we will receive His mercy, and find grace to help us when we need it most" (Heb. 4:15).

ALWAYS RUN TOWARDS GOD IN YOUR SIN AND WEAKNESS. Don't pretend. Practically speaking, the truth is sometimes when I am talking to God about what is going on in my life, I know I am doing something wrong or carrying a wrong attitude. But I am not yet ready to be sorry! I am not wanting to go a different direction. That may shock you, but I suspect sometimes most everyone is like me. We do not come to repentance easily.

I think we often avoid God when we aren't sorry and are not ready to change. We think we have to be sorry before we come to Him. That thought is wrong. It causes us to isolate.

The Bible says enter into His gates with thanksgiving. It's thanksgiving for who He is, for His love, for His commitment to work on our behalf. Enter in with full confidence that He is able to do all things, that He wants to be with us in our weakness. Think about it, our greatest strength is pretty weak, our purest thought not lily white when compared to His perfection. Don't come in pride, but in humble admission of where we are and we will find His presence there. It's nice if we are sorry, but in real relationships confession can come before repentance. Owning what we feel or do – top to bottom – is being transparent. Confession accompanied by pretending we are ready to change is not authentic. Don't do it. Instead of pretending – or avoiding – take your conversation with God deeper.

A proper reverence of God means we need to come willingly with our issues. Hiding from God is never a good policy. Rather turn yourself in. Tell Him you're guilty. The people I love most in life, the ones whom I naturally gravitate towards, are those who tell on themselves. I don't mean that in an unhealthy needy way that looks for attention. Rather they are simply open about where they are struggling even when that means they have done or are doing less than the ideal or the best. I feel like I can trust these folks because, rather than pretending they are all together, they value honesty above looking good in man's eyes.

Here are some things that can help your conversation with God your Father:
Don't just tell Him where you are, go deeper. Tell Him:
WHY you are not sorry.
WHY you don't want to change.
WHAT you are afraid of.
WHAT you feel like.
HOW you have suffered.
WHERE you feel/are inadequate.
WHO you are committed to serve.
HOW big, powerful and loving He is.

Explore your rebellion with God. My "I'm not sorry," conversations are very graphic. Telling God the why's for my lack of sorrow, the fears behind them, exploring the reason for my anger, the inadequacy of heart to meet a challenge, confessing the depth of my own sin. These need to be clearly painted before Him for our own sake, (He sees it more clearly than we do). What I have discovered about myself in these conversations sometimes shocks me! In doing this my own motives and wounds are discovered. In the telling, I let God be God. I am not His accuser nor His judge, even when I do not understand what is behind what has happened.

I may be angry, but I express anger in a way that stays mindful that He is God. God can handle profanity – it won't shake Him off His throne or change who He is, but I do not think it's helpful for us. I find it is a tool of the enemy. If you look at the most desperate, transparent prayers of David in the Psalms, there is no profanity. I assure you it is not because it was absent from the culture.

You needn't be afraid God will make you change! He won't MAKE you do anything. Instead, you will discover things about yourself. Your own roots of fear. Seeing and articulating these things make us want to change. He meets us where we are. He is just waiting for a crack in the door and a sincere invitation to enter. It is there He displays His greatest love, and He helps us trust Him with the outcome.

God is the one my heart is set on loving and serving. He is my loving Father. I am leaving my case in His hands. As far forward as I can "honestly" lean, I give Him permission to change me. God works most freely through permission. Be real about it. Sometimes the farthest I can lean is: I give you permission to change me, but I can't help you. When this is the case, my prayers can sound like this:

"I give you permission to change my heart because I really and truly want what you want. I also want you to know up front where I am. I don't think I can help you much in the 'changing my heart area.' I give you my permission, but you're the one with the hammer and chisel not me. You're the one who has the power to break my hardened heart. I also want you to know that I seriously want what you want. I hate living out of harmony with your heart. I just can't get there on my own. Come, Lord. Speak to me..."

Just a few words spoken from the mouth of God can not only change us, we can live off them for a very long time.

This is what I mean by deeper prayer. From my perspective, this type of prayer honors God and it honors my feelings. It is honest about what is behind where I am. It honors my relationship with God – that I am His servant, that I care about what He feels as much as He cares about what I feel. It expresses a desire to follow Him, an openness to change, and the depth of my own weakness and sin. I call it an authentic transparent prayer/relationship that lets God know that we both know where I am. It invites Him to be GOD in the midst of my weakness!

God answers this kind of prayer all of the time! He does it in ways we cannot guess. A changed heart is just that – changed. It is not a pretending heart. God changes our perspective more often than changing the circumstances (although he does that too). And sometimes changing our perspective is all the change the circumstance needs. At times it will be an aha moment. But at other times change has been so subtle, you honestly don't know when, how, or why it happened. The shift is often the doorway that ushers in His presence in the difficult/impossible situation. The bumpy, confusing, and crooked is made straight.

An Exercise in Listening.

Transparency is critical to building an intimate relationship. To love and be loved we must feel like the other knows and fully accepts who we are. Most everyone knows instinctively that God knows everything about them. Why then do we sometimes pretend in His presence? Are we ever not in His presence? Why do we become suddenly shy or overly confident, change our voice or use religious words? Why do we avoid

Him when we are not doing well? Is it because we think He want us to be something other than ourselves? That He wants a different version of ourselves, thinking the person we are makes Him uncomfortable? Is it that we want to be an idealized self so He will like us? Are we afraid we are going to do/say something wrong that will then offend Him?

If you have already resolved these kinds of issues, you are well into enjoying the benefits of partnership with Him. If not, I pose these questions for you to process in His presence. I do my best thinking as I write down my thoughts or speak them aloud. It makes them concrete. As you are thinking, invite God into your thoughts. See what happens. If I were a betting woman – I am not – I'd lay money down that He will speak to you. He so much desires to remove anything that would keep us from moving in the power of His love.

As soon as I saw you, I knew a grand adventure was about to happen.

WINNIE THE POOH

7

GOD ADVENTURES IN EVERYDAY LIFE

I love the book *Winnie the Pooh* by A.A. Milne. It was a favorite of my children and now of my grandchildren – particularly when read by my husband. He's a very good reader, capturing the voices and personalities of each character. He's spent a good deal of time as a student of these rich stories. When he reads them aloud, the adventures come alive in ways that delight the heart and teach the soul. Winnie can make an adventure out of the most mundane and ordinary of things, because as he says – "I'm just an ordinary bear."

And so it is with God's adventures. In His hands, we ordinary people encounter ordinary life and most anything can happen.

Adventures are filled with undefined encounters of things *not of our making*. Often we start out in control but then there is a twist that makes it special, sometimes in unwelcome ways. Like when my husband climbed Mt. Kenya with a few friends. They intentionally set out on an adventure, they prepared for what might happen, but were not in control of the details that turned the climb from ordinary into the extraordinary. One guy became so exhausted from lack of oxygen on the vertical bog that he begged the others to leave him in the freezing cold so he could "just sleep a bit and catch up later." They worked hard together to motivate and keep him moving by saying just take three more steps and then we will rest. Then they would count out the steps. It saved his life. They thought they had prepared for the nights spent in little wood huts out of the elements, but were sorely unprepared for an inescapable cold that permeated every cell of their exhausted bodies. Altitude sickness meant crawling from the hut to vomit outside. My husband contracted a tropical virus and had to hike down with 104+ temperature and developed an erratic heart beat as a result. It persisted for several years. Thankfully not all adventures are so radical or harrowing, nor so filled with such awe inspiring beauty.

Why would life with God not be an adventure? Certainly there are plenty of adventures that are not of God's making! Things we've needed rescue from. But putting your life in the hands of the one who created the Heavens and the Earth – now that is adventure in the making.

Having an "Attitude of Expectation" is the roadway WE lay down that welcomes Him into the "mundane of everyday life." After all, God didn't make life a long trek up Mt. Kenya. It consists of everyday routines of rising, preparing food, eating, working, eating again, rest, recreation, tending life, relating, loss, celebration, sleep, to rise again the next day.

There are some Mt. Kenya's along the way, but they are the exception. Expectation of God's presence creates a lifestyle of adventure that fosters worship, divine appointments, and enjoying and serving His presence in the midst of the mundane.

It came as a shock to me, but God created the mundane. I don't know why, but I thought life was always supposed to be full of very meaningful and stimulating excitement. I think it took the experience of having and raising children, to awaken me to the reality that God means the mundane to take up the bulk of our life. This was a major adjustment in my thinking.

Think about it – you do not want to live with your fingers in a high voltage socket. That is what high adventure is. It is very costly. It is living on the edge of insanity. (Raising kids is also costly and plenty of days you feel like you will go insane but it is different than doing 4 loads of laundry a day.) We can't take too much of it without suffering enormous consequences in body, mind and relationships. It is too stressful. It may be one of the reasons God does not tell us the details of our future. I have a friend who won a million dollars two times in the lottery. It led to his ruin. How would you like to live with that stress ahead of time? It was hard to live with as it played out. To rehearse it over and over ahead of the facts, torture!

If mundane is something made by God, then it must be good! I don't think God created mundane, however, to be boring! There are times I say, "Lord I could use a few weeks of boring."

It was never boring to go anywhere with my mother-in-love (law) named Dagmar. She was the parking queen. She never had a problem finding a parking space no matter where she was headed. She prayed first and expected God would open a spot for her where needed. Sure enough, **always** there would be a spot near her destination that seemed to welcome her arrival. I am not sure how this happened in the heavenly realm, but if you knew parking was going to be a problem, all you had to do was catch a ride with her and any anticipated problem you might have, vanished. Her supernatural gift for parking became legend in the family. It was fueled by prayer with expectation.

We miss so many adventures with God because we don't expect Him. We don't comprehend how much He loves to be with us in the mundane. Expecting His presence turns the ordinary into the extraordinary. You will do, hear, experience, and see things the crowds beside you miss.

If you are wise and you expect something to happen, you arm yourself ahead. Think about going to spend the day at the beach. You prepare for the sun, the water, the sand, hunger and thirst. That way you can enjoy the experience of the beach. If you are going on a vacation, you do the same. You think ahead about the weather so that you pack the appropriate clothing to keep you warm, cool and dry. You take your sports equipment, running shoes, books, and medications. You would feel yourself foolish had you not considered and prepared ahead. But in much of life we do not prepare for God's presence because we simply don't expect it. We live as if God were absent or occupied rather than with us.

Because I am in the habit of expecting God's presence, I prepare ahead. Let me give you some examples that may cause you to think me crazy. I always take note paper and a pen to the movies. I expect God to be with me, to speak to me... and who would want to miss what He might say? Guess what happens – He speaks!

We serve a God who is always talking – we just are not always listening. He is always teaching and encouraging, even in the movie theater. In a movie theater I feel I am often His audience of one. How rich is that! I do the same watching TV. He doesn't always speak, but I am always listening and I keep something near so I can write down what He might say. It takes little effort on my part. Because I believe God is always with me, I watch my program or movie with Him. If He wants to say something, I am listening and recording what He says. I do the same when I go to bed at night. I keep a notebook should He say something to me as I sleep. When I awake, I write it down so that I can capture and reflect on His night message. I keep my notebook in the bathroom so that I don't disturb my husband. Yes, that means I must get out of bed to write it down! I do the same in worship on a Sunday morning.

Expecting God to speak to me from the music, as I am singing to God, He'll let me hear His voice talking back about a phrase or idea. It makes worship a two way rich experience to be captured. The same happens in the message. I am tracking with the speaker and God will plop down and expand what the speaker is saying. God will emphasize something differently, expanding its meaning or speak deeply to my soul or imagination. I don't think my experience is unusual, I think this happens to most all of us tuned into a Sunday worship service. We notice it because we are paying attention. Coming to church with expectation make all the difference to what we hear.

What I am suggesting is you can live with that same sense of expectation all of the time. If you do, you will see God, you will hear Him, you'll have lots more adventures. Like Winnie the Pooh, adventure in the mundane will be a lifestyle rather than a place you visit.

I believe God likes to shop and save money. My husband says I have the gift of saving money! Of course to save money you have to spend money. That is the part he sometimes doesn't appreciate as much! Truly I expect God to be with me when I shop. I do not think of it as a waste of His time, because He loves to be with me, and He loves to help me use His money wisely. He also knows where the deals are. I know He will direct me to the right thing for the right price. In fact, I have often heard Him say that's too much, wait. I love to shop with God, I don't just talk to Him about helping me save money, I ask Him to help me find things that will bless others for just the right price. You may think this foolishness. I encourage you to try it before dismissing it.

I expect God to be with me in every disappointment. Once at the doctor's office I'd gotten a bad report on a routine blood test. The doctor stepped out of the office and feeling quite desperate I told God fairly loudly. "O GOD, YOU'VE GOT TO HELP ME WITH THIS!" I didn't realize how thin the walls were... that everyone heard my heart cry to God. When I came out, people looked concerned. A nurse asked if I was okay and told me about a support group at a local hospital. I shall never forget their look, and promised myself to be mindful of the thinness of the walls the next time I was feeling desperate at a doctor's office!

I love taking walks with God and noticing all the wonderful things that God has placed in our care. I enjoy the colors, the smells, the textures. I tell Him what an amazing artist He is. And I listen for His voice. I love taking headphones to the beach and worshiping God in music while I let His sunshine warm my body. He soothes my worries and energizes my soul. It wouldn't happen if I didn't prepare for His presence.

I watch for what He is doing around me. Who starts talking to me? Who responds to a question with a more lengthy answer when I ask, "How are you doing?" If they give me more than "fine," I consider it a lengthy answer. "Almost fine," "it's a bad day," "it's been a long day," "I'm sad," "been better," are all lengthy answers even though many only have 2 words! They are a sign that God is working in that person already. They are in tune with their emotions and God is creating a hunger in them for relief. Sometimes they will say, "Great!" Then I get to share in their joy. I see them as people in God's grip and they are deserving of a follow-up question delivered with a tone of concern or interest that comes from the love of God.

God is with me, He loves them, this is my expectation. RARELY, and I do mean RARELY, do they not respond. I listen, and then often we have a wonderful conversation. For those who are struggling, it is not unusual for them to tear up. I always offer to pray, because God is with me and with them. It is amazing what happens. The mundane turns into the extraordinary. I am often as encouraged by His presence as they are. Honestly even the one word answer "fine" you can work with... but it may not go anywhere. You can respond, "What is fine about your day?", or one of my favorite comments to fine is, "I consider fine a C on a report card. It's not a D, but things aren't GREAT. What could be better?"

Sometimes God uses this, sometimes not. It isn't because God isn't with me, but because He may not be resting on them at that time. It may not be their time. The worst that can happen is they will consider me nosey or at best a friendly person who cares.

When I go to a store that is closing (remember I like to shop and save money with God) I often engage with an employee by asking if they have found a new job. This always leads to a conversation. There is a desperate world around us and God wants all to know He is real, available and cares. I particularly remember two conversations. One was with a man who had applied to 14 different places and had not yet found a position. He had a child and pregnant wife at home. We talked about that. He was a non-practicing Catholic. He gladly stepped to a quiet isle and I prayed for a job. As he shed tears of gratitude he thanked me as God was gently calling him back into relationship. I reminded him he could talk to God that same way, anytime. Another was a gal who actually was desperate for a job. She not only followed me out of the store, but later I was able to bring her a bible and we prayed again. She told everyone in the store about her encounter with a "God woman." I got to meet a couple of them too. I was able to pray with her as she accepted Jesus. From time to time, my husband and I pray for people at a liquor store we visit for the wine tastings. In fact on occasion we have had employees tell their customers, "Oh, you should have Don and Nancy pray for you." They aren't suggesting it sarcastically either because we have prayed for them.

I had a friend once, who while waiting for her oil change in the waiting room of the local gas station, where the T.V. blares, was not alone. There was a young man also waiting for his car. The talk show airing was about S.T.D.'s. Suddenly the young man looked at my friend and said with some desperation in his voice, "I got a call yesterday from my doctor and he told me I have an S.T.D. I don't know how I am going to tell my girlfriend." Like most of us, my friend was stunned and felt very awkward. She said something like, "Oh, I am so sorry," and she fell silent. She wasn't expecting God's presence and wasn't prepared. A young man, in trouble, who so needed Jesus' love, didn't get it right then. It was a learning moment. How many times do we all miss God's invitation to speak because we are not prepared, we are uncomfortable, or we simply are in a hurry to return to our very important agenda. It is good to note, almost all adventures have an element of inconvenience and unfamiliarity.

I look for opportunities to engage with people in small meaningful ways, expecting God's presence. Do I look like a stalker? NO. Do I assault people with the gospel? NO. I look like a typical person out and about, because I am a typical person out and about! I don't appreciate stalkers. I do not appreciate people who are pushy. As Winnie the Pooh would say, "I'm just an ordinary bear." One who knows God loves every person! And I know people need to be listened too. Showing interest and truly listening to another even for 3 or 4 minutes often becomes a doorway of positive response when you ask them if you can pray for God to help them in their area of concern.

Does this happen every day? NO! If I gave myself to this more, I know for absolute certain it would! I, like you, often live life according to my agenda of the day. I work more than full time. My schedule has little margin for the unexpected. Expecting His presence is my lifestyle simply keeps me more aware. I believe everyone can do this. Expecting His presence is a highway in our brains that the Holy Spirit would love to lay down deeply. If I scheduled for the unexpected every day, if it was part of my agenda, I know it would happen much more instead of just regularly. As I reflect on this, I can feel God stirring my imagination with an invitation given to all: "Why not try?" "The harvest is plentiful but the laborers are few – pray to the Lord of the Harvest that He would send forth laborers into His Harvest fields" Luke 10:2. The Holy Spirit is the one who brings people to salvation. My part is to carry His heart, and plant seeds of love. I think of praying for someone as planting a seed. I get really excited when people say, "yes, please pray" because I know the Holy Spirit is right there. It gives them an experience of God's love and an invitation to experience more. We are God's invitation.

Making loving God the blueprint of your lifestyle is training yourself to expect His presence at all times, then preparing ahead for Holy Spirit encounters and adventures, remembering they are written on the everyday backdrop of the mundane tasks of life. I am reminded of this verse: "He who is faithful in little will also be faithful in much..." (Luke 16:10).

"As for God, His way is perfect. The Lord's words are flawless. He shields all who take refuge in Him."

PSALM 18:30

8

WHAT ABOUT THE BIBLE?

There are hundreds of thousands of Christians alive today with no idea of what God's word says. They live in regions of the world where it's not available. They have sovereign relationships of love with God, they follow Him they are close to Him, but they don't really know what He looks like. They would give anything to actually own a Bible. According to *Christianity Today* there are 6 countries where owning a Bible is very, very dangerous. To be found with one in your possession is automatic death or imprisonment. There are also 50 countries where being a Christian is synonymous with great persecution and access to the Bible is highly limited. In addition, there are about 2,000 people groups who have either no Bible or only partial portions of it in their own language. This part of our family doesn't know God's story in history. They are not friends with the people who have gone before us. They do not know the names of people like King David, whose lives have taught us about following God. Consider not knowing the stories of Jesus' days on earth or what He said as He encountered people. What if you didn't know what He taught nor heard of His miracles. To not know the heroines of our faith would leave great holes in my own heart. These people miss the experience of daily wrestling with God's word so they can be transformed by it. They cannot be accused of despising God by despising what His Word says because they have no option to have God's Word. God deals with them uniquely.

This cannot be said of us in the Western world. We have an abundant availability of access to God's Word. Christians often have multiple versions and copies of the Bible. Between my office and home I have nearly a dozen copies, plus I have the internet! The Bible is always within my grasp.

Yet, I have met numerous fellow Americans who don't have a Bible and have never seen one close up. And I've met lots of people who have seen a Bible, been in close proximity to it, but have never read it. I vividly remember a friend my boys brought home from school around Easter. Over dinner we asked him if he knew the Easter Story or how Jesus had died. "Not really – didn't one of His disciples shoot him?" was his response. This was over 35 years ago in America. We are surrounded with people who have never read a Bible. In Don and my travels in Europe, the same is true even though there is generally liberal access to the Bible.

If we have no "felt need" for God's Word, access makes no difference at all. We will not take time for things we don't need. We may as well live in a country where it isn't available.

It takes desire and hunger united to a will to prioritize time, to make use of the access we have. But this is not the end of the problems we sometimes encounter when it comes to God's precious Word.

At times our exposure to the Bible is to an older version that uses confusing language that keeps God at a distance through what seems to be "holy language." It can be hard to understand unless you are a poet who loves Shakespeare, or you are old enough to have grown up hearing and reading versions of the Bible which use thee's, thou's, arts, and lots of words ending in "th." The phrasing in these Bibles has not been used for hundreds of years. For most people today, these older versions seem like religious gibberish that simply doesn't make sense. Those who avoid them are not aware there are modern translations that are easy to access.

I shall not forget an experience I had while I was a patient in a hospital a few years back. A woman came in to do the routine cleaning of my room. She noticed I was engaged with a book and asked what I was reading. I responded, "The Bible." She promptly blew it off as uninteresting, then shared how she had tried reading the Bible many times but never understood what it said. I responded, "Really, what translation of the Bible do you have?" She didn't know. I said: "Let's do an experiment. See if you understand this one. I am going to open it randomly and start to read and you tell me if it makes sense to you." I do not recall the passage of scripture I opened to. I remember it was in the Old Testament. What I do vividly recall was the stunned look on her face. After a few minutes, she enthusiastically interrupted me and said, "That's a real Bible?" "Yes, it's a real genuine Bible," I answered. What she did next totally surprised me. She bolted across the room and grabbed it right out of my hands and began reading it for herself. She was in disbelief. With a big grin I asked, "Does it makes sense? Do you understand it?" She said, "This isn't like any Bible I have ever read. This DOES make sense!" Then she repeated, "This is a real Bible, right?" She was still in disbelief that the Bible could make sense. We had a wonderful conversation that ended in prayer. Then I gave her my Bible. It was a New Living Translation. She could not have been more excited because for the first time in her life, she heard God speaking though His word.

Understanding the Bible can simply be a matter of purchasing a version that uses modern language. The two I recommend are the

New Living Translation and the New International Version. Both are excellent at capturing the true meaning of the text with a voice that is contemporary and understandable. There are other versions that are excellent as well. You can go online and investigate for yourself. When purchasing books, they almost always let you peek inside to view what is written before you make a purchase. I am sure you will find "a genuine Bible" that makes sense to you. Should you prefer electronic books you can also make use of a copy via Kindle, your computer or an app on your cell phone, (Bible Gateway is a good one).

When God and His Word are not the center of our paradigms of life, the Bible is not the place we look for answers. We often do not assign to God's Word the value it holds. I am amazed how committed God is to helping us understand life, living, and who He is. His Word is living water but we are the ones who must drink.

In our culture today there is a growing pressure to see the Bible as out of date and not the word of God at all. Rather it is viewed as some people's ideas of what God said for the time in which it was written. Therefore it is irrelevant now because times have changed. More and more people believe this to be true, partly because the Bible is in conflict with our culture. This is particularly prevalent among younger generations but it also affects the older population. It is as true for those who attend church as those who don't. There is a secularization of the society that has invaded the church. Because of this, truths of the Bible are often dismissed.

There has also been much harm done to people and their faith, because of the scandals committed by those charged to represent God's Word. Pastors, priests, leaders and those who oversee them have committed grievous sin that is simply ignored or coved over. By their behavior they treated both God and His Word so disrespectfully that it proclaimed a message I know they did not intend to send: The Bible isn't true, God isn't sacred, His Word is not holy and it's not worth the paper it is written on. This is a terrible wrong – may God forgive us.

Our schools are adamantly opposed to the teachings of the Bible. Some teachers and staff believe in God, but dismiss many parts of the Bible. Young or old, if you subscribe to the cultural currents of today, it is easy to see the word of God as irrelevant to life now. It is certainly politically incorrect. Many think if Jesus were around today, He would say something different. Jesus and the Father are the same… yesterday, today and forever more. Cultures change but God remains the same. God may be outdated to our way of thinking, but He is not outdated to our time. His word is relevant to every generation. It will be expressed differently, but the heart of God has not changed. He is light years ahead of us, not tagging behind our cultural understandings of life.

If you believe in a God painted by our culture, it will be hard to encounter Him. You will be dismissive of His word and you will act as His judge. This is a very challenging place to find yourself in because it is backwards. God's Word is meant to judge us. It reveals who **we are** in comparison to God. It produces humility in us. One of the great strategies of the devil traced back to the first man and woman, is to convince us that we are equal with God. It says we are the center of the universe and can judge good from evil. To judge God requires great pride. There are times we judge God when certain things do not make sense to us. They seem unfair and unjust and therefore must be untrue.

There are many things I have not understood in the Bible. My lack of understanding does not make them less true. ***What it does reveal is that God and I are different.*** That should not surprise us, after all He is God….

By respecting that God is different and acknowledging the problem is not God, but our difference has allowed me to lay bothersome things aside for a season. I am a very visual person, so I think of this "laying aside" as a cabinet that contains a special shelf. (God often speaks to us through pictures.) I feel like God gave me this picture with this encouragement: He said, "This cabinet is a place you can safely store what you do not understand for another time." When I put my question on the "hold shelf" and close the door to the cabinet, the question doesn't disappear. I do not deny it, rather I know it is in safe keeping for another season. Like my summer clothes in winter, I store them with the confidence that a time is coming when they will be pulled out and ready to appreciate.

This exercise lets me be at peace. Un-answered questions do not torment me. They are not cluttering up my thinking or my faith. They do not keep me from moving ahead with God. I simply wait for God to turn on the light of my understanding. Because I do not deny or avoid these issues, I keep an eye out for clues. Some things I have understood within a short time; others took years of waiting and growing. I have been a Jesus follower for many decades. I have never retired my cabinet because I have not outgrown my need for it. It's seen a lot of use over the years. I have far less need for it now. The things I set in it now mostly have to do with circumstances I don't understand rather than theology. I long ago gave up my need to understand God's theology. I accept it. I wonder about it. I ask questions, but I also embrace that He is full of mystery, and I will not fully know Him till I see him face to face.

God loves our questions. They don't offend Him. I will never stop asking questions. Nearly every day I am asking questions. Never be afraid to ask Him for understanding. He delights in questions because they reveal a hunger to know Him, a hunger to grow. As children, there are somethings that are too big for us to wrap our mind around. So when we raise our kids we do the best we can to help them understand some things given their limitations. It is just the way it is.

Jesus said we must become as a child to enter His Kingdom (Matt. 18:3). There are lots of things too big for me. I see within time and circumstance. He is outside of both and is the creator of the universe – all things are held up by the power of His Word. It is a really significant and important difference. As my children trust me in spite of not always understanding me, I can trust God without understanding what is behind all He says. The other thing I do is embrace that my question is a starting point to understanding more about Him. It's a place of growing.

Both video and most board games have a launch pad, usually identified as the "START" space. I have found it very helpful to think of this as I consider my question. My "START" begins with this assumption: "God is always good and His ways are always true – there is no shadow or darkness in Him – He loves us" (1 John 1: 5). If that is your START, it directs your search very differently. *It takes the accusation out of the hunt* and makes for a positive quest! I think if you start anywhere else, you will have a much harder time gaining God's perspective on an issue, action He has taken or on what the Bible teaches.

This issue of how we handle questions is very important when it comes to valuing what God says. If we come as accusers we cut ourselves off from God by becoming His superior. We value our perspective as His judge. How we value something directs what we do about it. The value we assign directs our behavior. I have discovered there are two types of people: those who ask questions about God in order to dismiss Him, and those who ask questions to grow towards Him. They can be equally emotional in the asking, but will end in much different places. God can't resist those who ask questions to grow towards Him. It may take some time, but start by accepting His goodness and lean towards Him when you discover your differences.

Think about how Jesus valued scripture. We do not see Him questioning what it said. He depended on it to face the most intense challenges in His life. After 40 days of fasting in the wilderness, as He was being tempted by the devil to prove His divinity by turning stones into bread, Jesus didn't stand on His own, He didn't stand apart from God's Word – instead He stood ON God's Word.

He acted in harmony with it. God's Word and Jesus were joined as one:

> "Jesus answered, 'It is written: Man shall not live on bread alone, but on every word that comes from the mouth of God.'" (Matt. 4:4).

Each time the devil tested Him, Jesus stood ON God's Word. God's Word was central to Jesus action. It was His strength – it was how He was joined to God the Father. It was the ring of the covenant He wore that spoke of His unity with God the Father. Standing on God's Word and standing in God were one and the same. He understood that this was spiritual bread that was living. In it was life. It is why Jesus could say to Philip:

> "Have I been with you all this time Philip, and yet you still don't know who I am? Anyone who has seen me has seen the Father! So why are you asking me to show Him to you? Don't you believe that I am in the Father and the Father is in me? The words I speak are not my own, but my Father who lives in me does His work through me" (John 14: 9-10).

We often have not properly understood that words – all words – are alive. And that words reflect the inner character or identity of the person. "Out of the abundance of the heart the mouth speaks" (Matt. 12:34).

Think about this: what makes a kind person kind? It's two things: words spoken in kindness and love, and actions that are united or in harmony with the words. You cannot separate a person from their words. Words are alive and they reflect the person. It is true of spoken words and it is true of written words. They are very important to God. Jesus says we will be judged by every word we speak.

> "And I tell you this, you must give an account for every idle word you speak. The words you say will either ac-

quit you or condemn you" (Matt. 12:36-37).

God, (Father, Son and Holy Spirit) recognize this principle: what we speak is a revelation of who we are. Our words are not eternal, although their effect can have eternal consequences. The tongue holds the power of life and death (Proverbs 18:21). All of us have been on the receiving end of words that have both blessed and cursed us! And we've probably also both cursed and blessed others with our words. Thankfully, repentance is available. We say sorry to God and others and then live in harmony with our confession.

This principle – that we cannot be separated from our words that our identity is revealed through our words – is something that is true multiplied times in God. He is the one who came up with the idea... He reveals Himself in His Word – the Bible.

Yes! God's Word is as valuable as it is important. We can live without it, but we shouldn't, and we don't have to. When we do, we are missing a piece of God Himself that God meant us to have. In this day when people hunger to trace their ancestry to discover their identity, I pray we will have such a hunger to know God's identity and to discover our ancestors in the faith. I pray that their words and life will invest our world with meaning and that they will launch us into crazy and meaningful conversations with God our Maker, Father, and Friend. If we don't search for Him in His Word, we are in one sense living in a drought. But unlike natural droughts, this is of our own making. Water is all around us, but we simply do not drink it. We do not receive the life that is available, is eternal and will change not just us, but those around us.

God gives us His words so they can transform us. Through them He renews, directs, corrects, empowers, teaches, comforts, equips, feeds, sustains, and strengthens us. As His Word unites with the presence of His Spirit our focus and energy flow in new, contagious, expanded, life- giving directions. God uses them to affect the world around us – to reach out with his love to secure the lives of others for the kingdom. They carry the divine. How important is the bible! How alive are those words! Alive enough to scare the heck out of many countries who don't want the Kingdom of God let loose in their neck of the woods! The Bible is a revelation of God. It is alive; it's the gospel of good news that holds the power to change. Read it, and let it read you. Then live it, in a relationship with Jesus.

We have a choice. We make choices every day. We are accountable for them. This is my appeal to you. Spend a good deal of your life getting to know God in His Word. Meet with Him there. Do not accept that it is not understandable in spite of the fact that some things you won't understand immediately. He gave us His Word. He entrusted it as a gift by which we could know Him and grow in Him. His Spirit rides upon the wings of God's Word. He will not withhold himself from any person who is hungry to love Him. Make it a priority in your life. You will not regret it.

Here are just a few of multiple passages that list some of the things we can count on when we spend time with God and His Word:

> "For the word of God is alive and active. Sharper than any double edged sword. It penetrates even to dividing soul and spirit, joints and marrow. It judges the thoughts and attitudes of the heart" (Hebrews 4:12).

> "All scripture is God-Breathed and is useful for teaching, rebuking, correcting and training in righteousness, so that the servant of God may be thoroughly equipped for every good work" (2 Tim. 3:16-17).

> "Your word is a lamp for my feet, and a light for my path" (Psalm 119:105).

> "As for God, His way is perfect: The Lord's word is flawless; He shields all who take refuge in Him" (Psalm

18:30).

"Therefore everyone who hears these words of mine and puts them into practice is like a wise man who built his house on the rock" (Matt. 7:24).

"The unfolding of your words gives light. It gives understanding to the simple" (Psalm 119:130).

"For the word of the Lord is right and true; He is faithful in all He does" (Psalm 33:4).

"Whoever believes in me, as the Scripture has said, rivers of living water will flow from within them" (John 7:38).

"For the word gives wisdom; from His mouth come knowledge and understanding" (Proverbs 2:6).

"To the Jews who have believed Him, Jesus said, 'If you hold to my teaching, you are really my disciples. Then you will know the truth and the truth will set you free'" (John 8: 31-32).

"If you remain in me and my words remain in you, ask whatever you wish and it will be done for you" (John 15:7).

"I have hidden your word in my heart that I might not sin against you" (Psalm 119:11).

"So the word became human and made His home among us. He was full of unfailing love and faithfulness. And we have seen His glory, the glory of the Father's one and only Son" (John 1:14).

"For you have been born again, not of perishable seed but of the imperishable through the living and enduring word of God" (1 Peter 1:23).

"Turn my eyes from worthless things and give me life through your word."

KING DAVID - PSALM 119:17

9

BELIEF OR RELATIONSHIP

One of the most well-known people in the Bible is King David. He loved God deeply, lived in dependence on Him and his life reflected it. God identifies him as a man after His own heart. In his life, he had both wonderful and terrible seasons. Yet there was a time David managed to neglect his life with God to such an extent that it led him down a path to adultery and murder. This story is recorded in 2 Samuel chapter 11. In chapter 12, God confronts David with his sin.

If the man after God's own heart could end up so separated from his own values and the God he worshiped/knew/experienced to be real, it makes me question my own vulnerability. When the Lord confronted David through the prophet Nathan, here is what he asked David: "Why have you despised the word of the Lord and done this terrible deed?" God went on to say in the next sentence, "You have despised Me by taking Uriah's wife to be your own." Thus God connects how we treat His written Word to our "today" treatment of Him. And that should make us all take a deep breath.

I want you to know there have been many seasons where I have neglected God's Word, and thereby despised God. At the time I would not have put it in such terms, because I was not out committing adultery or murder. I was doing mostly basically good things. But my heart was not chasing after God first. It was distracted.

In God's mind to put anything above time with Him is to make Him less than that thing we have pursued first. We may not feel it is despising God, but we certainly are not honoring and worshipping Him. We may be making other things gods above Him.

My reason for neglecting God's word was primarily busyness. I intended to get to it – but whoops – day after day, week after week, month after month, the time slipped away and I was too tired, too busy, or too entitled to rest, to get to it. My belief IN God replaced my relationship WITH God. And at the time, it was something that I thought was good enough. Belief is never enough if it isn't united to relationship. It didn't work for David; it certainly won't work for us.

I'm not saying there aren't some good reasons for not taking time in God's word. I have had these seasons as well. Sometimes we are not capable. I had an operation that left me unable to put two thoughts together for at least 8 weeks. I was terrified, wondering if I would ever have a brain again. I have had other health issues that have set me back for periods of time (although sometimes those kinds of things drive us to His Word). There are times I was overcome by grief, or so busy with transition I could not focus on what God was saying. My relationship with God consisted of holding on through prayers for help. Times of crisis can last for a few weeks, months or much longer. Rather than reject us, God holds us close. They are often some of our most precious experiences with Him because we are wrapped and carried in His grace. I consider them holy.

When David slipped out of relationship with God, it wasn't during one of these holy seasons. David was in a neglectful and proud period of time. He'd worked hard for a long time and felt entitled to a bit of time off. It is a slippery slope to be found on. David substituted belief in God for a relationship with God, and was so unaware of this attitude shift, that when Nathan came and shared with him a story about himself, he didn't recognize that he was the villain. He had slipped so far away from God, he was guilty of things he NEVER could have imagined himself capable of. He was so disconnected from his own reality that he didn't recognize himself. That was the reason he became so angry at the villain and pronounced a very just judgment upon himself. He was living in self-deception and thought of himself as faithful, rather than the faithless servant he actually was. **This is the danger of belief not connected to relationship.**

Have you ever found yourself doing or saying things that shocked you because they were incongruent with your values in God? Things that actually reflected the work of the enemy. Something slips out of your mouth and you ask, where did that come from? I am sorry to say I have! When it happens I know I am in trouble – I know there is a disconnect. I still believe, but I know I have not been relating! When we take time to be honest with God, it forces us to be honest with ourselves. This disconnection is common in our busy worlds. When I have yet again been overcome by busyness and am catching God's Word as I can, rather than making conversation with Him over His Word the primary importance of my day – belief becomes elevated over relationship. It is just what happens. It's like brushing our teeth. If you don't do it every day… you reap the growing consequences. There is no avoiding them. When I haven't been taking time to enjoy God's presence, I find I can become like David: disconnected from what is really important. I can get by on belief, handle things on my own, and actually feel pretty good about myself.

Or when I am in a season of disappointment in God because He hasn't come through in the way I believed He would or should, I withdraw some portion of my heart from Him. Then I feel entitled to rehearse my wound or hurt. I've not stopped believing, I am just not yet wanting to have real conversation with Him, nor am I ready to spend time in His Word. I know if I do I will have to deal with myself. I haven't stopped believing; I've just stopped relating. This leads to our becoming stuck in bitterness.

How might we protect ourselves from traveling to where David did? How do we keep belief and relationship connected? How do we let God direct us from the worthless to the precious? These are great questions we should be asking ourselves.

As Christians, we usually embrace most of the Bible in our heart as true (while we may have some deep questions about some things). We believe that it has application for us and mankind. We embrace it as the revealed will of God in spite of some things we question. We desire to learn from it. We work at understanding what it means. These are excellent attitudes and values to have. I wish that all Jesus followers would ascribe to them! I believe however, this is simply Step 1. The danger of only doing this is we can keep the Bible at an arms distance, limiting its benefit to a manual for living rather than a LIVING manual. Living because it is God breathed – God is right there speaking today for those who look for Him. God is outside of time. The past, present and future are rolled into one. He lives in a different dimension with different laws. He supersedes time. We also have the Holy Spirit present to stir up new life in us. God, the creator of the universe, the holder and lover of our lives, is invested in His Word and uses it to invest Himself in us. If He removed the veil from our eyes, we would see an entirely different dimension before us. When we read His Word, keeping in mind that He is present with us as we read, it makes the reading of His Word a very different experience.

God our Father doesn't just want to take care of us. He doesn't want just to teach us. His chief aim is not to correct us. He wants to partner with us in His mission. He is concerned about relating to us. It's a forever together mission. He wants to bring His Kingdom to earth through us. Jesus said this is how to pray: "Your Kingdom come, Your will be done, here on earth as it is in heaven!" Jesus would not have commissioned us to ask if we weren't a key element to the fulfilling of the prayer. Being told to ask indicates the start of partnership; but it is not the end.

We can "up" our end of this partnership by approaching the Bible with our own words. I call this Step 2. Knowing God is with us as we read His Word, we can respond to what we think He is saying conversationally. (This morning as I was reading a passage I came upon something that challenged me. From another room, Don heard me say, "What is this about, God?")

We have an open invitation to meet with God over His Word. This is partnership. One of the things that makes great marriages, great families, great friendships and great work environments is the willingness of each participant to talk honestly and openly with the others, rather than keeping to themselves and avoiding conversation. It's a lifestyle choice. Why would we think partnership with our God our Father was any different?

David, one of my heroes, talked to God in this way. He didn't have the bible as we know it. He had the Pentateuch (first 5 books of the Old Testament) and most scholars believe probably the books of Joshua and Judges. But there is no question David knew and treasured God's words. He saw them as living. There is no doubt he talked to God about them. We have a record of his written and spoken conversations in the Psalms. I have chosen just very few of the many things David conversed with God about in the first 100 verses of Psalm 119. This psalm has 176 verses filled with more of these statements.

> "Oh that my actions would consistently reflect your decrees, then I will not be ashamed when I compare my life with your commands" (vv. 5-6).

"Your word have I hid in my heart that I might not sin against You" (v. 11).

"I study your commandments and reflect on your ways. I will delight in your decrees and not forget your word" (vv. 15-16).

"Open my eyes to see the wonderful truths in your instructions" (v.18).

"I weep with sorrow, encourage me by your word. Keep me from lying to myself, give me the privilege of knowing your instructions" (vv. 28-29).

"Lord give me your unfailing love, the salvation that you promised me. Then I can answer those who taunt me, for I trust in your word" (vv. 41-42).

"I used to wander off till you disciplined me; now I closely follow your word" (v. 67).

"May all who fear you find in me a cause for joy, for I have put my hope in your word" (v. 74).

"If your instructions had not sustained me with joy, I would have died in my misery" (v.92).

"Your commands make me wiser than my enemies, they are my constant guide. Yes I have more insight than my teachers for I am always thinking about your laws" (v. 98).

"How sweet your words are to me, they are sweeter than honey" (v. 100).

When we read the Psalms we sometimes forget they are simply conversations with God. They are primarily a record of his personal relationship with God rather than his belief in God. They certainly reflect that he had belief! As I read them I am encouraged, not just by his belief, but by how he translated it into transparent conversations. In the Psalms you can see David wrestling with God through the issues of His goodness and faithfulness, as well as his own confusion at the circumstances David finds himself in. His prayers/conversations are very real. It is one of the things that makes them so powerful.

I have always loved David! I am encouraged that God, who is outside of time, knowing there would be a serious lapse in David's relationship with Him says, he is a man after my own heart! I know if David could fall to such depths of sorrowful separation from God, we all are vulnerable and need to guard our souls. We have an enemy who would like to take us out. For me, guarding my relationship with God is paramount. It is simply not good enough to believe in God. It must translate into a lifestyle of relating. One of the most effective ways I have found of doing that is to make all my times with God conversational – that is two sided. That includes my reading of His Word. I talk with God about what He says. Sometimes it is out loud, sometimes it is written. But conversation for me is a must. When I talk to Him about what He is saying, it deepens my connection to Him. It is not an intellectual exercise of reading His word to know it – I am wanting to know the God who is using it to speak to me today.

If you talk to a wall, does it make the wall real? NO! Because it isn't a living being. God is alive. Talking to Him about what He says honors Him, acknowledges Him as living, and affirms Him as Lord. It also gives Him space by the Holy Spirit to answer either with words or impressions. I want to know Him more, and He wants to reveal more. When I am conversing with Him over what He says, it's wrestling with Him for the application and depth of meaning for my life, for my prayers, for understanding our world, for knowing how to relate to people around me, for having wisdom to do my jobs of pastoring, mentoring, mothering, being a wife, friending, neighboring and just about everything else. I want to be known as His eager student not just His child. And I want to be His friend. Jesus said I no longer call you servants but friends. I think Jesus means for all of us to be His friends.

What's required? Time. (Jesus became man. He worked as a carpenter. He understands the time it takes to do the mundane. He wants most of us to live life, not live in a monastery). Consistency is key to effective relationship. You also need a listening ear. Jesus said take care how you listen. How you listen reveals the difference between functioning in belief or in relationship. Some listen to give the appearance of being present when their mind is a million miles away. They listen, but do not hear. Others listen with heart and mind engaged, and listening leads to action. How you listen is a matter of life and death. A listening ear, an open mind and heart, a willingness to ask God questions, to dig deeper, stay in the conversation, to ask more questions looking for Him to direct your thoughts. We need the flexibility to be a learner, a willingness to reflect. All these are part of what it takes. Patience in the process is of utmost importance – but all of this is in the next chapter.

There is a difference between a relationship that has routine and one which becomes routine.

10
KEEPING IT FRESH

I f your times with God are stale and you can't make them work - ***shake it off, shake it off*** The issue is definitely not the raw material! The issue is probably **NOT** your lack of love or desire for God!

Notice how when you change things even a little – it grabs your attention. By adding some bold, some italics and changing the fonts, things feel different. Encountering God and His Word is like handling dynamite: there is power. Sometimes, however, it doesn't feel that way. You may just need to shake off what you are doing and change your routine to see it connect in your heart, mind, and world.

I've noticed when I get a new hair style, it makes me feel like a new person. I've just made a small adjustment, yet it often makes a huge difference. It can change the appearance of my features, how my clothes look, even how tall or thin I seem. Sometimes the difference is so dramatic it takes a few days or weeks for me to relax into.

Like old hairstyles, our routines or habits of relating to God can become boring. As long as they are filled with life they work well, but routine can also become a problem. Anyone who has been married any length of time knows this. When love becomes routine, it becomes stale. Sometimes tweaking things even a little gives an entirely new dynamic to the relationship. It's like adding a bit of lemon juice to food – it causes the flavor to sparkle. Employing new patterns of relating to God by stepping out of old ruts can add flavor to your life in Him.

Like any change there may be an awkward stage as we relax into the new pattern, but it can do wonders for freshening up our love for God. He is the always the same, but His love is unpredictable. Every sunrise is different. You never know what kind of flower may be delivered in His Name. If He always has fresh expressions of His Love, why should we not as well. There is nothing holy in doing things one way – particularly when it isn't working!

We are often taught that we should read the Bible and pray upon waking. This is the holy and accepted way to start your day. It IS a great way to begin a day! In different seasons of life however, it might be the worst time to read the Bible and pray because you have a new baby and are exhausted from being up all night!

Don't be afraid to abandon things that don't work.

Instead, I think of it this way: any time I meet God makes that time holy. The time is not what makes the difference, it's the person I am meeting. As far as I can tell, many of the times Jesus met His Father alone were in the middle of the night. Perhaps He considered that morning, but I, along with many others, can tell you from experience: night is a pretty great time to spend time with God. No one is around, no one will summon you on the phone, no meals have to be prepared. There is a stillness and therefore a clarity that is the fruit of the silence that surrounds you.

Don't be afraid to shake it up. When I am tired in the middle of the afternoon, drawing aside and opening my Bible for a Jesus conversation is much more refreshing and re-energizing than a cup of coffee or a quick nap! After a time with my Father, I am refocused and ready to go for the rest of the day. Not everyone has this luxury because of their schedule. I do, and I find it one of my most productive God conversation times!

I think of conversations with God as one of my Jesus "re-energizers." Jesus did nothing on His own. In our culture of independence this idea of doing nothing on our own can seem demeaning. If Jesus did it in His humanity, then I think that is a very good recommendation for us. I honestly can't imagine my life without Him at the center. It's why I've built my lifestyle around His presence.

I do my best when I am in partnership with God. I pray ahead, while I am in motion, and after the fact. In particularly stressful times I need to escape to spend extra time processing with Him. It doesn't need to be a lot of time but it does need to have a different type of intentionality. When I realize I am anxious or feeling insecure about something (usually something that is not in my control and involves some risk to me or those I love) putting it in His hands along with the specific fear I feel and listening to see if He has something to say or remind me of, goes a long way towards releasing me from the fear. Many times I heard the founder of the Vineyard Movement, John Wimber, say his greatest prayer was HELP! His second greatest prayer: HELP ME NOW!

Am I ALWAYS completely set free? Honestly, no. But God enables me to act against fear, and I have a peace to let go and let my heavenly Father determine outcomes. Truthfully, anxiety can be a sneaky little critter, so we don't often recognize it till we've overreacted, our stomach is upside down, our heart is beating fast, or our muscles are tied in knots. Whenever you become "aware" anxiety is resident, turn your heart towards Him and breathe out, letting go, then breath in the knowledge that He is with you no matter what... and listen for His voice. I say out loud, "Thank you Lord that you are with me, that you're ahead of me, behind me, beside me, above me and beneath me and that nothing surprises you!"

It's gonna be okay, even if the worse happens! Don't be afraid to escape for a few moments. A toilet stall works just fine as a prayer closet: and they are available in every office building, restaurant, doctor's office, store, etc. Sometimes we need to say things out loud to step towards trust in Him. Every once in a while fear bites all of us from behind!

Reading the Bible conversationally is another God re-energizer. It has been something I have done my entire life. I began as young child looking at pictures in a children's bible well before I could read. The pictures stirred me deeply and because, like many children, I simply believed God was real and with me, I naturally began talking to God about them. As an adult when I began reading the Bible to learn more deeply of God, I just as naturally began talking back to Him about the things I read. I seem to have been born this way. Prayer has never been unnatural to me.

I know this is not true for many. Often people begin their journey by observing God from a distance. They have been taught to be very respectful of God, and are uncomfortable about how to talk to Him. They believe there is "a proper way" to do it. Many don't want to disturb Him, thinking He has much more important business to attend to. They see their requests as puny compared to the very big and important things in the world. They are not convinced He would listen or respond. This genuine concern causes them to feel awkward as they approach God. God impacts them, but it is as if they are peeking through a hole in the fence at the neighbor's back yard. They whisper their prayers with down-turned eyes, embarrassed or ashamed rather than "coming boldly before the throne of our gracious God" (Hebrews 4:16). Knowing that God delights in the prayers of the upright (Proverbs 15:8), and that "the Lord delights in and honors His people" (Psalm 149:4). God wants them to know there are no fences in Jesus. He loves us before we ever love Him (Rom. 5:8).

I find those who read God's word conversationally and interactively are people who frequently share what God is doing, showing, and speaking to them in natural, non-attention-drawing ways. I believe this is because their life has become a reflection of their conversations. They mostly live in harmony with their conversation, whether it is in expressing the challenge before them, a failure they have encountered, the joy of some new understanding, or the confusion of not understanding the God "whose thoughts are not our thoughts." They are challenged in their thinking, energized by God's presence, and centered by their encounters with God – Father, Son and Holy Spirit. They have a natural healthy glow, not of their own making. It is a glow that transcends anger, sorrow, and disappointment.

I find it to be true of both extroverts and introverts. It is hard to keep a vital faith in God private – but they are not like neon signs, rather more like bubbling brooks. God's life is always percolating up in provocative remarks that tell you there is something going on beneath their surface. It is as true of them when they aren't talking directly about God as when they are. Their comments match the conversation – rather than a private agenda that sees people as a target to receive the gospel. Their everyday life with God (the ups and downs, the beautiful and the ugly) is the backdrop for their insights and experiences. If you talk to them for long enough some little gem from the Lord will appear in the conversation because they have been spending time loving Him.

For the majority of us, having this kind of relationship with God takes time. It grows rather than magically happens. When I was much younger there was a TV comedy titled "Bewitched." A normal looking young woman who had supernatural powers simply twitched her nose and whatever she desired would instantly happen. This is sometimes how we approach God. Our expectation can be that if we open the Bible and read a few passages it will instantly transform our hearts. It's much more complicated. Matt. 7: 24-26 reads:

> "Anyone who listens to my teaching and follows it is wise, like a person who builds a house on solid rock.... But anyone who hears my teaching and doesn't obey it is foolish, like a person who builds a house on sand....."

Both people listen but one responds by doing. Doing takes time. It incorporates failure, redoing and asking more questions. It is certainly not a routine. Obedience translates into experiences of or with God. They lead to deeper conversations. It takes time to experience God as a Father, the Holy Spirit as a teacher, Jesus as a Savior and brother. We are learning God: learning friendship with Him at the same time we are learning His Lordship. We experience His strength and power in the midst of experiencing our own weakness. A life story is being constructed that impacts heart, mind and life views. Every year our story grows bigger: understandings are stretched and revised as the friendship with Him grows deeper, and conversations grow freer, wider, and bolder.

Those who don't connect doing with hearing, miss the growing "experience" of God. They have a growing observation and theory of God in history that does them little practical good in life or crisis. It is deceptive. It creates an illusion of knowledge without truly knowing.

Here is what happens to most people who set about to meaningfully relate to God, through His Word. We open the book and a flood of 25 other distracting thoughts catch our attention. We don't understand what we read, we become very tired, get a text message or phone call! Everyone I know has had these experiences. When this happens it is wholly unsatisfying and demotivating. If it is a repetitive experience we give up OR we go through the routine of reading and praying in a distracted manner. We don't get anything out of our time with God in His Word. It's an empty, wasted, unsatisfying exercise that doesn't motivate us to joy or action. This is the experience of many people who genuinely love Him.

If the Bible does indeed contain everything that pertains to life and godliness, why would the devil not make disrupting our time with our Father a number one strategy against us? Are we going to let the devil win? Are we going to let our lives be robbed of the purpose, power, and joy that come out of time spent with Jesus? Are we going to miss the treasures that loving our Father, and Him loving us, deposit in our hearts and lives? Are we willing to let our sense of mission evaporate into the business of life? This is our choice to make. God will help us, but He won't make the decision for us.

There comes an age when your children – who will always be your children – become adults. As adults you respect their choices. You may not admire those choices but you do not tell them what to do. Instead, a wise parent loves, gives space, and waits to be invited to speak. We wait for them to ask because unsolicited advice is heard as criticism. Healthy people push those who criticize them away.

While you can't live another's life for them and many times it is not healthy to rescue, that does mean you are not in with both feet. Our commitment, however, isn't to control...it's to come alongside. So it is with our heavenly Father. He is all in, but He doesn't control. He will advise, come along side, and lends us the transforming power of His presence. This awesome mix of revelation, truth, and love bring about changes that would never otherwise happen.

I have discovered something about myself that you may also have noticed about yourself. If I enjoy something, if I feel it benefits me, I am much more likely to find time for it. There are lots of days I am so busy I forget to eat lunch, but generally speaking I MAKE time to eat 3 times a day because I love eating. I love the flavors, smells, and tastes of food. It makes me feel good. When I don't eat I feel terrible!

On the other hand, I don't enjoy exercise. I am not an endorphin loving runner. Even though it is very beneficial and I need it, I don't fit exercise in because it SEEMS boring and such a waste of time. It takes all the will power I can muster to add it to my routine of life. Unless I add fellowship as a distraction, I will likely skip it. It makes no difference how many times I tell myself it is good for me and will enhance my quality and length of life.

That is the way many of us think about our time with God and the Bible. If it is a lifeless routine, even though we know it to be essential, beneficial and will keep us going for the long haul. In our experience the short term reward is not worth the effort. This is our point of engagement in the war. It takes intentionality to defeat the enemy. Don't give up and don't settle for routine.

There are different types of time with God our Father. As disciples of Jesus, there are times when we might be in a small group, leading a group, teaching a class or preaching a sermon. We spend time with the Lord and the Bible to prepare to be a good participant, have something valuable to add to the conversation, or to give a biblical teaching. I call this **performance aimed** time with God. We are getting to "give". It's important. God speaks to us and changes us, gives us important messages for others, challenges us with life changing questions and insights. GOD calls us to do this kind of study, preparation, and prayer. I do not take it lightly, nor do I undervalue it. It is life changing! At the same time I want us to appreciate the motivating reason we invest in this type of "God time". It is so that we can give out to others. This is not bad – we need to do this because from these times, healthy community prospers. It is like the fellowship aspect I need to exercise. Everyone benefits.

There is another type of time with God. I call it *just for me* time – for my relationship with God. It is "getting to BE" time. There is a different deposit God makes in us during these times; and we make a different deposit towards Him. These are the times where He is working on my character, where He is wooing me and I am being vulnerable with Him, where we share secrets. He might reveal something about my heart.

These might be good and encouraging things, or not so good, somewhat discouraging things. It's a time where God reveals things about His own heart that are meant just for us. There is "us" time where I might just sit in His presence without words to simply enjoy being with Him... To un-clutter my mind and rest in His presence.

My husband is a fairly extreme introvert. I too get energy from being alone. We like to take drives. We can easily drive for 4 hours and not say one word to each other. We just enjoy being together, finding it very restful. Words would clutter up our time of quiet enjoyment together. Each of us is free to talk, but we are just as content and comfortable with the silence. It is extremely refreshing. My "quiet" times with God are like this. I am aware of God's presence and His deep pleasure in me, on me, and of me. It transcends words. I am resting and being refreshed in His presence. I am sometimes quietly thinking before Him, sort of silently exploring a thought. At other times I am not thinking at all, like my head is empty and I am being quietly carried. I imagine it would be more difficult to do this if you were an extrovert. A few of my grandsons are hyperactive. They can't sit still and have to move or be engaged. Inactivity drives them crazy. When you sit next to them in a meeting, you'll notice their foot or leg is always moving. God made them this way. He is not angry that they have sparks of electricity always firing. Their time with God will look different than mine.

Jesus spent lots of "just for me" time with His Father. We see it when He repeatedly draws away to be with Him at night or in the early morning. He leaves His disciples and goes off into the mountains alone. Those were "just for them" times of conversation, quiet reflection, being alone, and of loving each other. Out of them we know Jesus drew energy, direction, and strength to stay on mission and to do what the Father was doing.

Time with God leads to our convictions about God. Convictions hold us in crisis and in trouble. Convictions empower us. Yes, it is God holding us and empowering us, but conviction is key. Convictions are faith in action. I am not a theologian, I don't understand what it means for Jesus to be fully God and fully man. But I think Jesus's personal times with God were crucial to His Father forming Himself inside the fully man part of Jesus. I believe it was out this that He gave Himself to God and to us. I think out of those times – in full humanity – He walked on water, multiplied loaves and fish, raised Lazarus from the dead, quieted raging storms. I think this because if He didn't do this as a man, He couldn't charge us, as mere men, to do the same things. Yet this is what He did.

We want to make sure we have both "getting to GIVE" and "getting to BE" times with God as we build a lifestyle of loving Him. We need healthy community and heathy community is aided immensely by heathy individuals. We can believe that because we spend *"getting to give"* time with God we are fine, not realizing that *"just for me"* time with God is actually more important because it is where a depth of strength, security, authenticity in relationship, and authority is born. It is foundational to relationship. Ultimately it is out of that deposit we can most give to others. Yet this is the kind of time with God that we can easily neglect. This type of prayer boasts of an audience of one. It is in adoring Him alone that a more intimate love is nurtured.

Before you read the next chapter – I'd like you to consider making a commitment to your Lord and Father. If for any reason you find yourself in a season of avoiding spending "just for me" time with Him, simply tell Him you are sorry and that you want Him to help you make some changes. Be honest about why you think you avoid Him and ask Him to reveal any hidden reasons beneath this avoidance.

If your "just for me" time is stale or has become routine, ask God to help you try some new things. Commit to stick with them long enough to see if they are a "fit" for you. You have to be willing to go through an awkward time of getting used to a new feeling or experience.

John Steinbeck once said, "It's a hard thing to leave any deeply routine life, even if you hate it." Patterns of relating sometimes get laid in concrete and we need God to pry us loose. Remember, routine isn't bad if it is working. Life is full of helpful routines. It is bad if routines become lifeless ruts. If your time in His Word feels like a lifeless rut, ask God to dislodge you. Do some experimenting. Let God know you're ready for a new adventure in the Holy Spirit.

There are two primary choice in life: to accept conditions as they exist, or accept the responsibility for changing them.

DENIS WHITLEY

11
GROWING

C hange is hard and it's uncomfortable. As a result it's not something we generally rush towards. John Maxwell says: "People change when they hurt enough they have to change, learn enough they desire to change, receive enough they can change." I find this insight very helpful because it sets change in the context of a person's current life experience.

Growth and change are partners. Change can lead to growth and growth can lead to change. How do these two work together in your spiritual life? If you think about spiritual growth, it is not something we generate on our own. Jesus tells us in John Chapter 15, He is the vine and we the branches. To grow we must be rooted in Him, receiving the life that being connected to the vine generates. Our job is to stay connected. His part is to give us sustenance. His intention is fruit. We can do nothing of value on our own. Yet unless we expend effort to develop patterns of connection that are meaningful, there will be no sinews of connection that allow fruit to grow.

I was once at a Christian Leaders' meeting, where one of the speakers shared about their devotional life. As I listened to them my thought was: Wow do they have connections! "They should be writing a book about loving God, not me!" It was a very humbling experience. Their devotional life was very different than mine. It sounded like they spend at least 2 to 3 hours daily in disciplined structured prayer. They have prayer in the morning, afternoon and evening. They do multiple regular spiritual exercises, and spend times away at spiritual retreats and silent retreats. They pray regularly for all of the people they love and are responsible for (it's a lot of people), and pray for bigger world matters. The fruits of these practices are evident in their life. They are clearly rooted in the vine! The speaker was not advocating we all do exactly as they do – nor boasting of their God life. They were simply sharing what a typical day/year of developing their inner life connection to God is like. It was a demonstrated example of how they are seriously pursuing being Jesus disciple. They are a wonderful, inspiring, and a great model of what a life lived in relationship with God can be like. We need more people like them who will share on how they grow and live in God.

Yet, I couldn't at this time in my life, maintain all they do. I was inspired and encouraged yet I also thought, this recipe would not work for me. While listening I was also tempted to be dismissive of my own life in God. As I struggled with those thoughts, I realized it was because I had fallen into the trap called "comparison." This person had much to teach, but not each lesson could be applied to each person in the same manner. I am positive that was not their intent.

Resist comparisons, unless it is for the purpose of praising another! You are not them. There is something in each of us that loves to compare. Be forewarned, as you head down that road, there are two ditches you are likely to end up in. You will dismiss what you are doing as not great enough and you'll despise what God is doing in you (which is what I was tempted to do). Or you will think I am doing so much more than them, and end in self-praise, looking down on another and falling into pride. One of my favorite Nancy-isms as I consider the work I do and the faith I have is: "there will always be people who do better than me and always people who don't do as well." I take great comfort from this thought because it is so true. The issue isn't better or worse, it is faithfulness and effort, plus functioning in who you are. The speaker I had listened to thrives on structure. I also thrive on structure applied to certain things, particularly when learning something new. But once I've learned it structure feels stifling. More creative in nature, I thrive on integration that is free spirited and integrated into everything. My husband is different than me. Both of us together, get a lot done.

Don't compare. Be yourself! Find what works for you, love what God is doing in you and keep hungering for more of Him. Don't be afraid to stretch into the unfamiliar (growth), but resist comparisons, because in the comparing sin will likely bite you in the behind.

God invented community so we can learn from one another. It is good to stretch. Never think someone who is different does not have something valuable to add to your life. They have things you need. Yet God has made each of us uniquely and we all have seasons and personalities appointed by Him. In addition He has gifted each of us differently. We do not have the same propensities towards the same activities. I know people who have written a worship song every day to God. It is a part of their lifestyle of loving Him. I haven't. I do not have the gift of song writing. Although I am artistic, I don't have the same sensitivity or gifting as those who are *highly* artistic. I know people who having this gift and sensitivity, with great devotion, employ it in their lifestyle of loving God. I know a young woman who has told me she never feels God's presence more than when she plays drums. It is part of her lifestyle of expressing and receiving His love. How silly it would be for me to compare myself to them. I am so glad God has the enjoyment of their connection to Him each day. They have enriched heaven's environment in ways I have not. They have enriched my life by their great devotion and service to Him. In the Bible, King David had a song writing gift. We are blessed to have His songs (psalms) that remain with us. They encourage every generation's heart connection to God. Don't dismiss who you are because you are different than someone else you highly esteem. God speaks both in silence and in sound. You may hear Him more clearly spending more time in one discipline than another. Some are aided by lots of structure, others by more freedom. Seasons can change just like our taste buds. So experimenting is a good thing. And who wants french fries every night except kids. I prefer a varied menu both in my foods and in my ways of loving God.

To be a true disciple means we are apprentices/students of Jesus. We can't learn our craft outside of relationship with Him. Jesus knows us and treats us accordingly. He is teaching us in the ways we learn best. Think of it this way: there is only one way not to cut off your finger with a saw. We must keep it clear of the blade!!! Yet there are many ways to hold timber so that you keep your fingers free of the blade. I have a unique way of holding a crochet hook and of doing cross stitch. I don't seem to be able to do it exactly the same way as others. However the fruit of my labors is as beautiful as those who do it "the right way." Connection to Jesus – being in Him – living as His student is the key. That means there will be certain shared skills, but how they are acquired or expressed maybe unique to the individual. Not all of you will take a pencil and paper to the movie theater so you can write down what God tells you... yet for me it is a tried and true way of hearing from God. I am also pretty certain this is absolutely the only book where you'll find this spiritual discipline mentioned. I hope you'll see both the humor and lesson in it.

Growing in each of the seasons God brings our way, at whatever level of experience we have, with whatever gifts God has currently given us, is a matter of choice. If we are not satisfied with the level of relationship we have with our Heavenly Father, if we hunger for more, we are the ones responsible for pursuing change.

Because we are made in the image of God, it means we are made with the power to create. God won't steal this from us. He honors us by letting us carry the responsibility of creating our relationship with Him. Whatever we invest or create on our side, He will meet. He is the great multiplier.

This is found throughout the Bible. Abraham's child, Isaac, is not solely an individual. He is the beginning of the fulfilment of multiplication that God promised Abraham that would be "as many as the stars in the heaven, and the sand of the sea." Isaac's son, Jacob, becomes 12 tribes. Jesus begins with 12 disciples who turn the world around and are the founders of the church. Theirs stories and words by the power of the Holy Spirit are still impacting us today. Jesus as one man, goes to the cross, and in so doing purchases a multitude of people in time. We see God has written this about His heart in nature. One acorn or pine cone lead to a forrest. My point is this: God reveals Himself as the one who multiplies. And in Zachariah 4:10, He tells us not to despise the day of small beginnings.

When we think of creating our life in God, remember we are partnering with the one who multiplies even our smallest efforts! "God who is able through his mighty work within us, will accomplish infinitely more than we might ask or think" (Eph. 3:20).

I have done many things to "create" my life in God. Most important is to make myself available. That means simply showing up to meet Him, in the good and bad times. Often the bad times are the easiest to show up in, because we are so desperate. Then there are the REALLY BAD TIMES. There was one year in my life where I was so low spiritually, I didn't know who God was. He was certainly not who I had believed Him to be. I felt everything I knew about God had been stripped from me. I could not bring myself to even read the Bible. In addition I was recovering from surgery and had young children, so I was depleted physically. My "showing up" was comprised of Don (my husband) reading a devotional book to me each day. I would let him pray for me, mostly because I was so confused about God I didn't have faith to pray to Him myself. I went to church because I knew it was good to be where God was. These were willful acts of availability.

Seriously, is that creating a devotional life with God? Yes it is, if that is where you are. God didn't despise that small beginning. God met me there and more than quadrupled my willingness to sincerely show up. To this day I do not understand how or when it happened, but in that year He totally transformed my understanding of who He was. And it was a very GOOD change. He rebuilt my understanding of His nature.

There were times in my life where my heart felt numb or dull. Every life has mountain tops and valleys. Showing up and "creating my life in the valley" has more than once been comprised of picking up a pen and writing out a few verses of scripture, then talking to God in no uncertain terms about them. I don't understand this... I don't believe this... you haven't done this... why do you say this? I'd like you to do this in me...

I took myself by the scruff of the neck and by my will made myself respond to God because I believe He is God – whether I am in a good place or not. I believe He loves me whether I feel it or not. I have often done it with little expectation of return. As I've done this over a few weeks (sometimes just days) my heart has always thawed and I discover I have grown. Remember, God multiplies what we do!

Most all of the tools I use to foster my love connection to God have two shared elements. The first is conversation. I have talked a lot about this in the previous chapters. I talk out loud, even if it's a whisper, or I talk on paper. Sometimes I do both at the same time. There is something wonderful about expelling your breath in prayer. It involves more than your head. A pen in hand has the same power. It is doing something active. Typing on a computer and watching my words appear on a screen works well for me too. As I am typing I will talk out loud and tell God how wonderful the things He is showing me are. I must expend some type of energy. I would love to be able to paint or draw my prayers. God appreciates the language of color, shape, and forms. His handiwork is on display all around us. If I were more gifted as an artist I would surely employ this language in prayer.

There are times when I have simply written love letters to God. I have had seasons where I did prayer walks outside every day. And if the weather was bad I prayer walked at the indoor mall. I have prayed through devotional books, and systematically prayed through the Psalms and Proverbs many times. I have done journaling. When I had a house full of babies and dishwashers were not yet an everyday essential, I prayed three times a day, as I washed dishes.

I've spent seasons getting up in the middle of the night to talk to God when all is quiet. I still regularly pray at night usually around 3 am. Now I don't get up. I just pray as I lay in bed. Missing sleep to pray has never made me more tired – unless it was to pull a special all-nighter! Jesus often prayed in the night or early morning hours before the world had awakened. And He retreated to pray. This alone time is very important.

I've done brooding prayer (meditation). I like calling it brooding prayer because I quietly turn a passage over and over again in my mind throughout a day brooding over it, watching to see what understanding emerges over time.

Another element of my "just God and me time" is focused on Scripture. I love God's Word. To read it is to hear His voice in a very personal way. It is like it is a diving board from which I leap into His presence. Currently God and I are conversing our way through the Bible – Him the teacher, me the student. I have been at this for over 3 years.

All these forms of communication have been of great benefit. There are many blueprints for fostering a lifestyle of loving God. I am not advocating one way of encountering God as life-giving over another. What I am saying is if you are stuck in a rut, avoiding time with God and the Bible because you find it boring, you can't focus, or it seems un-beneficial, there are many things you might try. Just pick something and give it a chance to grow on you.

Here are some simple keys I have put together that can help you get on a different footing.

Key 1. Make a time and place. This is the biggest thing that stops us from getting started. Try to be alone. This is a challenge with young children. By the time you find time to be alone you want to nap. So as I said, my alone time was with my hands in a sink of dirty dishes and my kids occupied with Mr. Rogers or Sesame Street. When I had just one child it was when I put them in a stroller and walked and prayed or sang. One man in our church drives to a cemetery because that is the one place he feels like he isn't going to be distracted or self-conscious. I have the ability to close out a crowd of people, so sometimes I've been known to plop myself down in a food court with my Bible and a pen and paper. This allowed me to be away from the office, the house, the phone, and my chores.

Key 2. When you meet with God and read His Word, treat the Bible like it is alive and treat Him like He is with you. If you do, He will be there. His Holy Spirit will stir your heart. He is more real than the environment surrounding you. Can you imagine someone talking to you (remember God's Word is alive and active) but you just sit there dumb, mouth closed, mind turned off. Don't be guilty of checking out. Engage with God. Talk back to Him and keep your ears and mind open. He will talk back and also guide your thoughts down paths you'd not imagined. Your expectation is like gold in the bank. It pays dividends. God enjoys being treated like He is present. It creates a platform that welcomes Him to speak.

Keep it active. If you are active, try walking, running, writing, typing, singing, painting, or doing dishes. It will keep you focused. You cannot nod off nor are your thoughts as likely to wander. I had a friend who when running every day took a page from the bible and memorized it as he ran – then he'd talk to God about it. There are exercises that include breathing, using your body, and engaging your imagination that all aid in staying active – engaging physically in what you are doing spiritually.

I share what follows as an example to stimulate your imagination of how you might communicate in your own unique way with your heavenly Father. It is not a model to be copied. You and I are different so what is real for me would be fake for you. If you were to watch me pray at my computer, you'd find my eyes closed, typing, then my eyes open reviewing our conversation. At any point I might be talking out loud, closing my eyes again as I think and talk more deeply exploring our passage together. You might hear me telling God how brilliant He is. You'd surely hear me asking questions. God wants you to engage your senses. They help you pay attention. Don't be afraid to use your imagination and step into the scene. As God speaks back to you write down what He says. Use it for more conversation. I sometimes find myself crying. Frequently I laugh out loud and often I smile. I verbalize the joke or the joy with God. Sometimes what He says will stop you dead in your tracks. It will be prophetic in nature and it is no time to talk, rather just receive. Those times are particularly important to record so you don't forget them. Store them somewhere special so you know where to go to find them.

Key 3. Slow it down. You don't have to be in hurry or travel a long way. Speed can be a huge distraction to intimacy. Think about this in the same way you would think about walking verses driving. When you walk you see and savor things you never notice when driving at 55 mph.

Go for deep and also wide. Panorama views of what is happening inspire a different type of awe. I love them as they give me the broad perspective of God's story. You never want to limit yourself to only talking to God about the details. It's like looking at a feather under a microscope without ever enjoying the vision of the entire bird. It is a bit foolish.

I travel to Spain regularly. There are so many panoramas I love. Three of my many favorites are, first, outside the old city of Toledo. The second is in Granada, overlooking the Alhambra from the surrounding hills, or from inside the palace in the Alhambra, overlooking the city. The third is from a park that sits on a mountain overlooking Barcelona. All of them are breathtaking, and hard to wrap your mind around. I love praying for big things when I stand in these places. I could stare over the beauty they display for hours. Always, when I am in these places there is a quiet that fills my soul. I become aware of God's bigness and my own insignificance. God's compassion takes hold of my heart in a very special way that causes my prayers to often be mixed with tears. History and time flood my heart as does the vastness of the task of God's mission and our utter dependence on His faithfulness to see any of it accomplished.

It is an entirely different experience to walk the streets of Toledo, Granada, or Barcelona. Then you touch the commerce, the personality, the sounds, the people both young and old, the friendliness, the creativity, the foods and smells that invite you to know that place more intimately. Every street reveals new treasures to be discovered or enjoyed. There are people to meet and conversations to be had. It's there I touch in a different way, the heart of these cities. It's there I love something that is tangible. It fills me with unspeakable joy. The panorama makes me feel small like a single thread in a big tapestry. Then walking the streets one step at a time, makes me feel the importance and impact one person can have – what it means to connect.

We need both for the sake of knowing intimately. Slowing down works better for me. Think of God's word in this way. If you let your mind rest on one phrase of one verse and talk with God about that, you have created an impactful moment with God. Your experience of Him has expanded. His presence has guided you into discovering something new about yourself, about the past. You have discovered something more about the people who have gone before you, what they thought, how they lived. That relates to the people around you now. Eating God's word in little bites, certain can be more life changing than skating over the surface of an entire chapter or book of the Bible to move onto another pond or panorama the next day.

It is my conviction that unless you regularly slowdown in order to interact with God as you read His word (panorama or bite), you are performing an intellectual or spiritual "duty exercise." You won't remember what you've read and you are not likely to be changed as deeply by His presence.

Key 4. Panorama or bite, write down what you observed. Which verses stand out to you? Anything that doesn't stand out to you simply lay aside for later or for another time entirely. Focus on the things God's Spirit is resting on. What stands out to you may be a promise you need at that moment, something you don't understand, something that jumps off the page as true, or something you are seeing from a different angle or for the first time. I am often riveted by things that seem out of place or don't make sense. They cause me to read and re-read and re-read again asking God what is going on. It may be a story, word or phrase that grabs you or causes you to ask a question of God or yourself. Let your conversation rest there. These are learning moments. I am the student and I come as a servant. I call this conversational reading.

Pay attention to the thoughts, pictures, words or other passages that come to mind. This is usually God talking back to you. Engage with them/Him rather than just moving along. Mine them for they contain silver and gold. Take some time to read through Proverbs 3. It has to do with listening to wisdom, embracing her, trusting God, and the benefits of pursuing a life of loving God. Remember, God talks. As children, our job is to listen.

Key 5. Respond. Turn what you've heard or learned back into intercession for yourself, your land, your neighbors, your enemies, your church, your family, your world, the people you love, the people you work with. I find writing my prayer down is a way of staying with my prayer to its end. In my experience, Key 4 and 5 usually happen somewhat simultaneously. But if this is new to you, it is often helpful to separate the two.

Here are some other things that are helpful:

Stop when you have run out of time. God isn't judging you. He is glad for the time you took, not angry that you didn't take more time. If you feel guilty that the time you took is not enough, you'll not spend any time at all. Does that make sense? Is no time better than some time?
Tomorrow is another day. It takes a lifetime to discover who God is. If we live to be 125, it still would not be long enough to know Him as He is. We will not truly know Him till we see Him face to face. Unless Jesus comes soon, we will not have that experience until we step into eternity. We surely will not be free of all the filters that influence us till then. And should we live 125 years, there will still be more people to pray for, and events to invite His presence into. It doesn't rest all on one person's shoulders. God is moving amongst the many. Just bring what you have to the party.

Stay with a book of the Bible until you finish it. This allows you to lay a stronger foundation. If it takes you 4 days, 4 weeks or 4 months – so what. The important thing is that you have encountered God and been changed, not that you read the Bible in one year (I have done this numerous times so I'm not against it). Remember you are building both a lifestyle and a lifetime of "growing encounters" with God.

Regularly read Psalms and Proverbs. Proverbs are wisdom bullets. They are short, intense, black and white, and loaded with insights for living. Psalms are prayers of true dependence on God in all kinds of situations. They lend perspective on how to marry the emotions of praise and discouragement of circumstances. I read from a New Testament book or an Old Testament book every day. I change it out doing my New Testament book one day the Old Testament the next. I also regularly read Proverbs and Psalms.

When you miss a day or two (or a week), just get back on track. Life is unpredictable. Don't beat yourself up. Repent when needed and start again. Try not to let weeks turn into months! I am currently in a group who do this together. Not everyone meets with God in this way every day. Some do, but everyone would love to do it every day. It's a pattern you develop. Everyone aims to do it 3 times weekly. We've a non-intrusive, non-judgmental way of letting a point person know that we're taking time to intentionally engage with God's Word. It encourages us all to keep at what each one of us knows is important. It is a life-giving discipline we do not want to let slip in our lives. Amongst these gals it feels like I give or get a little kiss from God that says your time with Me is important. We help one another remember that He is listening for our voice and He has things He wants to speak to encourage us. We need one another. I need non-judgmental accountability that doesn't criticize or feel invasive. It is a wonderful asset of community. Internet makes community available to all. Our group has people in it from 3 different states. It has been international at times. Distance, time, and circumstances fade from the list of reasons we might feel alone. It's not the only thing each of us does. We have accountability in our local church community as well. It is an easy to get in and easy to get out of group.

Let me end this chapter by encouraging you if you do not already do it, to add conversational prayer to the blueprint of your lifestyle of worship. If you do it regularly you'll discover you will start treating God like He is with you all of the time. Your Father will become your closest friend. You'll find repentance not only comes much more quickly, it is easier. You'll discover His presence and His Word resting in your heart, giving you counsel and comfort as you walk through everyday life.

I will not tell you how long or short the way will be only that it lies across a river. But do not fear that, for I am the great Bridge Builder.

The Voyage of the Dawn Treader by C. S. Lewis

12
ADOPTED IN lOVE - A JOURNEY OF CHANGE

As I bring this book to a close it is fitting I am writing today. I have a dear friend and co-worker in the Kingdom who with her husband made a decision to adopt a child. She had never parented before. She was 47 at the time, her husband 51. They took in a foster child who was almost 2 with the intent to go through the adoption process. Today they are in court to finalize that process and will leave the court as his official true parents. She recalls with tears the first day he came to live with them. He was asleep and she was standing over his crib. She reached down to caress his head and back and heard God say "he is yours." From that moment she was smitten by an overwhelming love for this little stranger.

She is an amazing lady. Divorced many years ago after a heartbreaking marriage, she married her second husband about 9 years ago. Attractive and brilliant, with a spectacular work history, and a distinguished spiritual resume in New Age, she began attending our church with him after they married. Because of her husband's love and respect, and hearing the gospel for the first time, she was touched by the Holy Spirit, became convinced that Christianity was not just true but that Jesus was worthy of her life commitment. She became a follower of Jesus.

When she and her husband married, they owned a two seater convertible sports car and an antique Trans Am, and a third car. During the warm summer and fall months in New England, they would cruise into the parking lot in the sports car, roof down, big smiles on their faces. All was well in their world. All of us would smile at the joy they were basking in as a newly married, free as a bird, couple. Many of us were slightly jealous. They could go anywhere they wanted. Each highly responsible, they had the freedom financially that most don't enjoy. Her being 6 ft. tall, a highly fashion conscious beauty, she always looked casually elegant and was the envy of every teenage girl in our church.

When the baby came along they sold the beloved sports car – no room for the baby! Their wings were clipped because they were only allowed to have pre-approved babysitters stay with the child. She curtailed one of her jobs in order to care for this active toddler. Their budget was hit, she started sporting a more casual look, leaving out the elegant part because how can you be elegant around the clock with a 2 year old? They put the antique Trans Am on the market because, "We just don't drive it anymore. It's not practical."

They are both on my hero list! Talk about a lifestyle change! Everything about their life is different. When they married they purchased an older home. They did a lot of work rehabbing it. By the time the baby came, the inside of their home looked like it was one of the feature stories from Better Homes and Gardens. Today, it looks like a home that is occupied by an active 4 year old, still lovely, just occupied. Eating out with the boy now happens in family friendly restaurants that are much less expensive.

Have the changes been easy? Not exactly! In fact it has been one of the most challenging things she has ever done. And she will tell you in no uncertain terms that she has learned why people have children in their younger years. But when you ask her if she'd do it again, she'd tell you, "Yes, in a heartbeat." You see she is in love with this little guy who is a bundle of energy, brilliant, stubborn, and has some challenges when it comes to accepting boundaries.

I share her story because it is not easy to give up one lifestyle for another. Giving up freedom for discipline is to surrender being self-directed towards what feels good or urgent at the moment. Don't we deserve a little self-comfort? Yes... as long as you agree that God's idea of comfort and yours might be just a little different. Our appetite must get used to a new menu. Once it does, the old flavors lose their appeal.

My friend would tell you it has been very hard, but that it has also bonded her to her husband, to this little son, and to God in a way nothing else could. There is something about coming into contact with our limitations that can cause us to need God in ways that we've not been aware of in the past. In these places a new lifestyle can be born.

My hope and prayer is that this book will be read by many different kinds of people. That in the reading all might walk away with some little gem from God, that would encourage them to grow towards loving Him more – every day in every season – in authentic natural ways.

Whenever we are making changes there is a process of incorporation. Some changes are made more easily, others come with time – all require intentionality. I always tell people who are making changes to any aspect of life – think 3 to 5 years down the road. Where do you want to be then? Yes in one year you will be different – but not as different as you'd hoped. In 5 years you will have seen areas you didn't think could change, transformed – in 15 years people might not recognize the person you have become as things that once were mighty struggles will no longer be issues at all.

In our culture of instant everything. We have lost the sense of change taking time. We get on an airplane and in 12 to 14 hours we can be on the other side of the world! I can go online and not just talk to someone but actually see them, in a distant land in a matter of seconds. On our cellphone we carry an entire library of information that we can access at the push of a button. It is unreal! We bring that appetite and expectation of instant gratification to things that need time to grow.

I have been working on growing a lifestyle of loving God for as long as I can remember. It has taken almost more failure than success, persistence, trying again, resolve to discover new ways of enjoying and including Him in my every day, all my seasons of life. I've had a commitment to keep it natural and real. That has been combined with a sincere love and devotion to God. I don't know why this has always been important to me – but it is behind the life I have in Him today.

I've needed to keep reminding myself: God wants to celebrate my successes not focus on my failures. I've reminded myself of this so often that at some point I began believing it was true. God loves us! Every time you partner with Him, He is thrilled. He is like my friend who looked for the first time at her little soon to be son sleeping, and heard God say: "he is yours." She was smitten with love for a stranger! It was a love with no explanation. God's love has no explanation either, it cannot be quenched by our failure, stubbornness, active mind and body, or our willful disobedience. It isn't stopped because we gravitate towards self-satisfaction and self-centeredness. It is not hindered by the brokenness that we inherited from life's hurts or the sense of unworthiness that chases us down every day and night. God looks right past those things to the fact that we belongs to Him. There is something unexplainable in the mystery of that connection.

Love takes time to work its charm. There are so many good things in each of us that God's presence and love want to uncover. His presence is good for us. It's Him at work doing a creative miracle. He is building and transforming us for not just this life but the one to come. We are a joy to Him. Fellowship with Him is so valuable He died to secure it.

Make loving God the blueprint of your lifestyle. It's a rich and meaningful way to live. Enjoy being close to Him. He enjoys being close to you. You are not alone. The challenge is worth the work, you will not be sorry. You will not come to the end of your life and say – I wish I had spent less time with God.

When we live in relationship with God – Father, Son and Holy Spirit, we live in the presence of eternity. God in us. God with us. God saving us. God changing us. God forever delighting in and loving us, through thick and thin.

We are practicing for eternity.

CONCLUSION

Isaiah 55

I conclude with a chapter written by the finger of God through the prophet Isaiah. It contains an invitation to come, an oath that He'll meet you beyond your wildest expectations, and a revelation of your purpose and destiny to not just live in eternal joy and peace, but to display His great glory now and forever.

"Is anyone thirsty? Come and drink – even if you have no money!
Come, take your choice of wine or milk – it's all free!
Why spend your money on food that does not give you strength?
Why pay for food that does you no good?
Listen to me, and you will eat what is good.
You will enjoy the finest food.

"Come to me with your ears wide open.
Listen, and you will find life.
I will make an everlasting covenant with you.
I will give you all the unfailing love I promised to David.
See how I used him to display my power among the peoples.
I made him a leader among the nations.
You will also command nations you do not know and peoples
unknown to you will come running to obey, because
I the Lord your God, the Holy One of Israel,
have made you glorious."

Seek the Lord while you can find Him.
Call on Him now while He is near.
Let the wicked change their ways and banish
the very thought of doing wrong.
Let them turn to the Lord that He may have mercy on them.

Yes, turn to our God, for He will forgive generously.

"My thoughts are nothing like your thoughts," says the Lord.
"And my ways are far beyond anything you could imagine.
For just as the heavens are higher than the earth,
so my ways are higher than your ways
and my thoughts higher than your thoughts."

"The rain and snow come down
from the heavens
and stay on the ground to water the earth.
They cause the grain to grow, producing seed for
the farmer and bread for the hungry.
It is the same with my word.
I send it out, and it always produces fruit.
It will accomplish all I want it to, and it will prosper
everywhere I send it.
You will live in joy and peace.
The mountains and hills will burst into song,
and the trees of the field will clap their hands!
Where once there were thorns, cypress trees will grow.
Where nettles grew, myrtles will sprout up.
These events will bring great honor to the LORD'S name,
they will be an everlasting sign of His power and love."

Printed in Great Britain
by Amazon